THE WIVES' TALES

the good, the bad, and the really ugly.

COMPILED BY

YASMIN WALTER

written by FIFO wives for FIFO wives.

Edited by Tracey Regan
Interior design by Dylan Ingram & Chelsea Wilcox

 A catalogue record for this
work is available from the
NATIONAL
LIBRARY National Library of Australia
OF AUSTRALIA

National Library of Australia Catalogue-in-Publication data:
The FIFO Wives' Tales/Yasmin Walter

ISBN: 978-0-6451353-3-6
(Paperback)

ISBN: 978-0-6451353-4-3
(eBook)

THE FIFO WIVES' TALES

the good, the bad, and the really ugly.

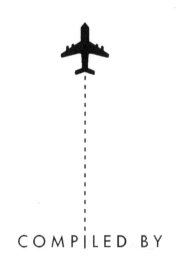

COMPILED BY

YASMIN WALTER

written by FIFO wives for FIFO wives.

CONTENTS

fifo

ACRONYM

FLY-IN FLY-OUT. IF YOU ARE A FIFO WORKER YOU GENERALLY LIVE A
LONG DISTANCE FROM YOUR WORKING SITE.

"MY HUSBAND WORKS FIFO"

SYNONYMS: *CASHED UP, RICH AF, SINGLE MUM, CHEATING HUSBAND,
ENVY, MY HUSBAND COULD NEVER LEAVE HIS FAMILY*

Hey you. Yeah you … thanks for picking up this book. Before
we jump into the good, the bad and the really ugly stories of
FIFO life, I thought I'd give you a bit of a back story as to why
I thought it was crucial this book was published.

As a FIFO wife myself, I'm part of numerous support groups
on Facebook, filled with women who want to talk about a lifestyle their nine-to-five friends and family just don't understand.
Every second post is a cry for help. Women are looking to lean
on other women who are also navigating the FIFO gravy train.
There are ups and downs to this lucrative lifestyle - BUT it does
often come at a cost.

The purpose of this book is to spark a conversation for FIFO
families and their networks, to give them a better understanding
of what being a FIFO spouse really entails. Everyone has an opinion on the lifestyle, but unless you are a part of it, you have little
actual knowledge on how challenging the balancing act is. We
want to provide current, past and future wives, girlfriends, sisters,
daughters, and mother-in-laws, (and the list goes on) access to

real life experiences they can relate to, and find inspiration and guidance from individuals who are dealing with similar situations.

Since putting the call out for real-life FIFO stories, we received over 300 expressions of interest. We really appreciate the hundreds of people who are willing to share their stories. All contributors were carefully selected to bring to the readers the best possible combination of the good, the bad and the really ugly. Some are still happily in the industry and others have withdrawn on unfortunate terms. We've included both the positive and the negative experiences. The concept behind the book is not to scare families away from the FIFO life, as there are many wonderful benefits in the industry, but I want women, in particular, to know that their sacrifice has not gone unnoticed, and there are families out there experiencing the same fears, joys and uncertainty.

Throughout the stories, there is a common theme that FIFO is not for the faint-hearted. And it is absolutely not for everyone. It's difficult, yet equally rewarding if you can find the correct balance. In this book, we discuss EVERYTHING - and I mean everything. From tears on fly out day, to juggling the kids and home, on-site affairs, and substance abuse, and then tears of joy on fly in day, having dad at home for two weeks straight and, until COVID at least, the spontaneous holidays. Whilst each family has their differences, they all still experience a lot of 'misses.' Missed birthdays, missed anniversaries, missed celebrations, missed achievements, missed births and miscarriages. From all the stories submitted, I have concluded that people are hungry for support, and this is on both sides of the family unit. The book showcases the point of view from everyone involved; the FIFO worker, the spouse, the children and even the ex-wife, or two.

We hope these stories will inspire you, support you through your journey, encourage open communication and hopefully bring a smile to your face.

Get to know us, I promise we're fun!
🄵 🄾 @thefifowives
Join the conversation - connect with The FIFO Wives' support group on Facebook.
BLOG + SHOP www.thefifowives.com

The FIFO Wives' community is a safe haven for those seeking support whilst in the fly-in fly-out lifestyle.

We share our wins and we share our pains - in a judgement-free zone.

'ADAPTABILITY IS KEY. WHILST WE OFTEN RESIST CHANGE, CHANGE IS INEVITABLE. IN THIS LIFESTYLE, THE MOST SUCCESSFUL RELATIONSHIPS DON'T COME FROM THE STRONGEST OR THE MOST INTELLIGENT PEOPLE. THEY COME FROM THOSE THAT HOLD A DEGREE OF FLEXIBILITY, TO ADAPT TO WHATEVER LIFE THROWS AT THEM. CHANGE THE WAY YOU THINK TO ACCEPT NEW BLESSINGS.'

Yasmin Walter – 'The CEO Wife'

THE CEO WIFE

NAME: YASMIN WALTER
INDUSTRY: OFFSHORE OIL & GAS
RELATIONSHIP STATUS: MARRIED 10 YEARS
TIME IN INDUSTRY: 11 YEARS

'Pregnant mother raped and stabbed to death as young daughter slept next to her.' That is how I thought this swing was going to end, and this was going to be my life summed up in a headline. Paranoia, fear and pregnancy hormones had been working actively to feed my obsession with crime shows. But to be fair (because I swear I'm not actually that crazy …), in the line of work hubby is in, he gets paid a prettier penny for engaging in risky work. A couple swings prior, there was a fatality and a poor father was caught in strong winds, which caused a shipping container to crush him. I was seven months pregnant, kissing my husband goodbye for three weeks with my three-year-old hanging off me bawling her eyes out. All of our emotions were highly strung at that moment, but my tears of sadness quickly turned into tears of disgust as my morning sickness was still going strong. A one-way ticket to the toilet for me and a one-way ticket to the middle of the ocean for him.

That night I was realllllly on one. I had created multiple

psychotic scenarios in my head. And you know, FIFO Murphy's Law is that when hubby is away, shit hits the fan. So I'm in bed trying to wind down and stupidly I check my local community page. Why did I do that? Because I wanted to check if there was a murderer making rounds tonight. I mean obviously it would be posted on that page. First post, Karen complaining about her neighbour's bin wheel on her driveway. Fuck it Karen have a 'like.' Next post 'WARNING ...' Ah fuck here we go. Ted Bundy (well an Aussie version anyways) is back. 'I just had a lady knock on my door asking to use my phone. Luckily for me I have a camera and I could see a man attempting to hide behind my neighbour's bush. I have a speaker on my camera and asked her leave. I've called the cops.' GREAT!! Love this for me. Did I get off Facebook? Of course I didn't. Next post from my general feed this time ... 'REMEMBER TO CLOSE YOUR GARAGE DOOR ...' FML here we go again. 'Boyfriend leaves house for under an hour to pick up dinner, he accidently leaves the garage open with his girlfriend at home. An intruder walks in and rapes his girlfriend. Be careful ladies!'

> **Survival #1:** Keep him in the loop, they need to still feel included. Everybody says communication is key, however I can confidently say it is the TOP tip to surviving this lifestyle. I often find myself having one sided conversations for most of the day, but once he clocks off, he appreciates all the texts, pictures, videos and voice memos from his family.

Perfect! I'm home alone, pregnant, a toddler to take care of and I have no security cameras. Do you now understand my hectic front page news headline? Lol. Now it's time to triple check that I've locked up and put a stick thing in the track of every door and window, the garage is completely shut, my bat is up against the wall, my pepper spray is in arm's reach and my door stopper is jammed in from the inside. Between trying to avoid a home invasion and thinking my husband was going to die, I started to plan a life without him and how I would raise the girls on my own. Crazy I know. What additional business I could start, even though I already have many successful income funnels. Do I remember that 500 number code for the crypto account? Who's going to take the bin out? I then pictured my eldest daughter getting married and her daddy not being by her side. And who's going to be by my side if it's not the tall dark and handsome guy that I said 'I do' to (I could slide into Chris Brown's DMs, I mean he does have yellow fever, wait sorry, I digress). I'm going to blame the pregnancy hormones (because you're never going to see a Cancerian weak) but I was lying in bed, hugging my daughter in an inconsolable, (think Kim K ugly cry face) fit. Then what do you know - cop sirens start blaring around my estate. Cool, I think I'm now safe but also who are they chasing and why?! A murderer?! My sister's ex that I have a VRO on? One of my best friends is the Chief Crime Reporter for a news station here in Perth, so she would unwillingly be on speed dial to calm my nerves. If I heard a helicopter circling, cop sirens wailing, hell even a dog barking, she would know why. So of course, I texted her at midnight and she replied instantly, 'Car chase, go to sleep babe.' Now that I think of it, she responded way too fast. I think she may have told me some porkies because she knows how I get. What a good friend.

Now the distance situation wasn't new to us. In our first year of marriage I was at an all-time low point in my life on the brink of depression. We were kicked out of our rental that we shared with my mum, sister and her boyfriend. The owner wanted to move his kids in, so we went searching for our new home. We couldn't find anything suitable to accommodate all our needs within the deadline so my family separated. Hubby and I ended up living with another best friend, on the floor of an unused living room; no door just our mattress, a TV and stacks of clothes on the floor. I grew up in public housing and I've been in and out of women's refuges, escaping a childhood of domestic violence from my mother's new partner. I've lived in dire states and had sleepless nights of uncertainty, but this definitely hit me differently. When I was younger I knew I had no control of my situation, my unhappiness was circumstantial. Yet being essentially homeless, due to choices I made, was not a good feeling. During this time, I was being flown to Sydney frequently to DJ, one of many job titles I've accumulated over time. You name it, I have a business card for it somewhere. It was at one of these events that I met my future business partner and now really close friend. Sydney is buzzing with entrepreneurs, hopeful (and broken) dreams, hustlers and most importantly, restaurants that didn't close at 10 pm. Once I packed the decks up it was back to Perth to continue my mental downward spiral. I would cry, randomly. I couldn't help it. I didn't even know why I was crying. My friend would see me, and her heart would drop, looking more helpless than me. She would prepare me a bubble bath and my husband would carry me in. He would stroke my hair and my face saying gross sweet things.

> Survival #2: Stay busy. Visit friends, visit family, just do you boo. I'm actually highly productive when hubby is away, especially with work. I guess when you don't have to allocate time to cuddling you can actually get shit done. Is wife guilt a thing?

I picked up some temp work for a mining company to save some money for our overseas wedding. Call it luck or the universe aligning us on our path, but it was through a connection I made there that hubby was able to attend an exclusive, fast track training course to be a coded welder and secure a really good placement offshore. 'You should move to Sydney, Bee,' (my pet name). 'It makes you happy there. You can try the business idea you have. You can fly back whenever you want, I can visit you there. I don't want to see you cry anymore.' Within a month, his first fly-out date was set and I conned my friend I was living with, to make the big move with me. She hated me for a week and refused to talk to me. Fast forward ten years and that bitch won't move back lol! God I miss her. Sydney was a good move. Like really good. I was motivated. Inspired. Stopped crying. I was happy and kicking goals. But I missed my man. Terribly. We had our own random fly-in fly-out schedules and we made it work. We are both so fiercely independent, and this definitely worked in our favour as we lived on opposite sides of the country.

> **Survival #3: Act your wage and spend wisely. This is a very lucrative industry and also an unpredictable one. Have a budget, make a plan and stick to it. Don't be a statistic and get stuck in the loop of FIFO with nothing to show but a last season's Louis Vuitton bag, a petrol guzzling loaded car, a wanky boat and an unaffordable mortgage.**

Being away from your partner is so important. It sounds scary but it's actually a good thing. It helps you grow individually and independently. Life is all about balance, looking forward to seeing your partner and missing them helps you realise how much you value your relationship, and your partner. It's imperative to enjoy your own interests, your own friends and indulge in some me time (even if that does mean a good trashy TV binge. Boy do I love those … Am I right?) Not to mention how much shit you get done. When hubby's not home, I can focus on my work, run a tight ship with the kids, do the visiting rounds and not feel guilty for staying up on the computer (like I am right now to type this), when he goes to sleep alone in our bed. But remember, you are the main source of your happiness and your family's happiness. When mummy's happy, generally speaking, everyone else is happy. So don't lose yourself! Turn time alone into a positive experience.

This FIFO lifestyle naturally means that sometimes, dad's going to miss out on celebrations too. Sure most events can be redone, like birthdays, Christmas etc., but finding out you're pregnant, after six months of trying and hubby is on his second day of a three-week swing, is not one of them. It was our first child. It didn't feel right to tell him over the phone, so I waited. There were so many times I wanted to blurt it out when we spoke. My cheeks would start to hurt from trying to fight off a big cheesy excited grin. And finally it was fly-in day. Woohoo. Aht, aht don't start celebrating yet. 'Flight delayed by two hours' said the annoying text he sent. I thought ok, what's another two hours. So now I'm at the airport and all the FIFO wives are parked up on the strip leading to the airport. No matter how much money our men are earning, us cheapskates refuse to pay for airport parking. 'We've landed but they said we can't get off for twenty minutes.' The excitement immediately turned into frustration, well borderline anger. Forty minutes and about a hundred laps later, he came out. Instead of being happy to see my sexy baby daddy I said, 'You took fucking long enough.' Poor guy was at the brunt of my frustration when he had no control of the situation. Let's just blame it on the pregnancy hormones again, I swear I'm a nice person. I snapped out of my mood pretty quickly and caught myself doing that stupid cheesy grin again only this time, he could see me, and that stupid cheesy grin. He asked, 'What are you doing?' haha! I played dumb and was saved by a phone call from my mum. We had his best friend's birthday party that night, we were already running late and I didn't want to rush the moment. By the time we got home, he was too drunk so I waited until the morning. I thought I'd be cute and make a puzzle that read 'I can't wait to meet my daddy' and it totally went over his head #pinterestfail. Forty-two weeks and a thirty-six hour labour later, our beautiful sumo baby girl was born.

Misconception #1: 'The money it provides is going to make you happy.'

There are many issues that can arise from the FIFO life and fertility issues are high on that list. It was time to add to our brood, however it's easier said than done. My cycle wasn't regular since I gave birth and neither was his roster. Hubby stepped down from a regular stint to focus on a degree in Psychology and Counselling (which he has now graduated from and is full steam into his Masters of Psychology and Psychotherapy). As controlling as I like to be, this was just one of those things completely out of my control. After two years of trying, false alarms and heartbreak, we were blessed with another beautiful girl. Gushing girl mum over here! I was in the midst of Kalgoorlie Fashion Week, an event I produce in regional Western Australia, when I started to feel sick and suddenly found myself vomiting. I began to get flashbacks of morning sickness from my last pregnancy and I just knew I was pregnant. But then again, I didn't want to get ahead of myself. The last time I peed on a stick after four months of no menstruation, Aunt Flo decided to visit on my stick. How's that for a fuck you and your uterus? I told hubby, 'I think I'm pregnant,' which kind of fell on deaf ears because I had been saying it for the last two years. It wasn't until he heard me vomiting that his eyes beamed with excitement and he went straight to Coles supermarket and returned with eight pregnancy tests. He said, 'No fancy announcements this time just show me the stick.' And BOOM ... I've never been so excited to see two stupid little lines. I couldn't believe it.

As the FIFO game goes, fly-out dates are never confirmed until you are on the plane. There was a big project pending that hubby was specifically sourced for and the potential fly-out date was anxiously dancing around my due date. Did I mention we sold our house and moved a week before I gave birth? Yeah, well we did. I like to keep our life thrilling like that lol. I just needed her to hold on for one more week. I was probably doing more lifting and shifting than I should have but I'm not one to just sit back and watch. And like the good little girl she is, she waited until mama had finished unpacking and styling before she made her entrance on her due date. I said to hubby that morning, 'You better finish painting this room because I'm having this baby today.' His dad laughed it off with him. An eighteen-hour labour and three failed epidurals later (that's six needles in my back for those counting, we can't forget about the good old pre-needle needle), our second princess was born.

> **Misconception #2: 'FIFO breaks families' - It is not a causal relationship. It's people's efforts to navigate and communicate the FIFO lifestyle which breaks up the family.**

Honestly she was three hours old when he got the call we had all been trying to avoid. He was flying out the next day. In the FIFO game, when you've made the exclusive 'go-to' list and you decline a swing, the next person moves up and you get bumped off, for good. 'I got this,' I said. 'I've had a newborn before, I've got mum staying with me, I got this.' Turns out I don't got this. I breastfed my first daughter for two years so I thought it would be second nature when I fed this one. She latched on beautifully, she was sucking perfectly, and milk was over-flowing but she was constantly crying and lethargic. A few days later it clicked, she hasn't been having as many wet nappies as a newborn should. I rang the child health clinic and they sent a nurse immediately. We weighed her, then I fed her under the nurse's supervision for ten minutes. She was satisfied with our performance so she weighed the baby. She had put on zero grams. Yep not even 0.01 of a gram. I expressed some milk and she downed the entire bottle. I went numb. I had been starving this poor baby for a week. When I tell you my heart shattered in a million pieces, I'm not even exaggerating. My helpless child was relying on me to keep her alive, but I was failing her. How stupid was I not to pick this up earlier. I was all alone. My mum was at work. My husband was at work. I had no energy and was too embarrassed to reach out to anyone else for help. I called hubby, which was pointless because I couldn't talk. He felt terrible. Terrible because he wasn't here, terrible that I was beating myself up over it and terrible that the poor baby had been starving. He did his best to reassure me I was doing a good job and he was thankful for what I'm doing for the girls, but that didn't sink in. I mean why should I believe it? I had no one else to blame but me. I went to three different specialists and no one could diagnose what was wrong. Fast forward to twenty months, most of which she was milk obese from mum over compensating, I have finally stopped exclusively pumping. It was like having a part-time job. Pump, wash, feed repeat … eight times a day! I pumped for 9,600 hours. That's 400 days or fifty-six weeks. Hubby is happy to have his milk bar back.

> Misconception #3: 'FIFO breeds toxic masculinity' - Tough working conditions demand a tough mindset. It is the inability to switch off the tough mindset, that influences toxic masculinity when it also serves as a defence against social anxiety.

As I said above, I am financially independent and I manage multiple businesses whilst parenting full time. Contrary to the mainstream belief, you can have kids and still be a boss bitch. I work when my kids are sleeping or at school, allowing me to be financially and physically present for them. And the same goes for dad. On hubby's off swings, he doesn't slack off. When he is home, he is home and is completely hands on; with the kids, myself, the house work, heck he is often persuaded to rock freshly painted toenails every now and then too thanks to my eldest #girldad.

Do I love the FIFO lifestyle? Like anything it has its ups and downs, but if I had to answer yes or no, it would be yes. But it's not something I recommend for everyone, or as a long-term plan. This industry has allowed us to set up our lives financially, yet with the flexibility of choice and freedom. Spontaneous holiday? Why not. Movie night during the day? Why not. Let the kids have the day off school so we can go to the cuddly farm? Why not. At the same time, do I feel lonely? Yes, when I go to bed alone. Do I feel like a single mum? Absolutely, especially during school prep and showers before bed. Is it sad when he misses special occasions? Of course, particularly the kids' birthdays. To survive this lifestyle you have to be mentally strong, be disciplined with your earnings and have very open communication. And most importantly, have an end goal.

'IT'S A TOUGH LIFE ABOVE GROUND AND UNDERGROUND. WE WORK AS A TEAM WHETHER WE ARE NEAR OR FAR. STRENGTH, RESILIENCE AND AN UNCONDITIONAL LOVE OF OUR FAMILY IS KEY. FIERCE INDEPENDENCE AND A GREAT DEAL OF BRAVERY KEEPS THE DREAM ALIVE.'

Alix Andriani – 'The Cougar Wife'

THE COUGAR WIFE

NAME: ALIX ANDRIANI
INDUSTRY: MINING
RELATIONSHIP STATUS: MARRIED
TIME IN INDUSTRY: 4.5 YEARS

I am a wife, a mother, a daughter, a sister and an aunty (all my favourite titles). I drink a ton of coffee and back it up with wine. I love reading and serial killer podcasts. I am a fine scotch and taco enthusiast. I dabble in amateur photography and my family hates my photoshoots. I am a hairstylist and my mum thinks I'm pretty good. I hate pasta, chardonnay, AFL and judgemental people. I love pineapple on pizza, Harry Potter, the crèche ladies at the gym and Mark McGowan. Nothing makes me happier than perfectly ironed clothes (thanks dad), smashed avo and my sons' fresh cuts. Family and friends are the key to a good life.

If you ask me, FIFO life saved our marriage.

My husband and I met at the gym nearly eight years ago. Sounds like a cliché but he was definitely perving on my squatting technique and I certainly couldn't look past those sexy arms in that red singlet. We bumped into each other one night, and well the rest is history. He did forget to mention one little detail however, he is six years younger than me. There is some truth in being a cougar. Guys like a woman who knows what they want, there is less drama and I know I will always have a sexy toy boy.

Survival #1: Don't Sweat the Small Stuff.

The first year of our relationship was hot; we broke a bed, bought a block of land and got engaged. The only way to describe our second year together was absolute beautiful madness; we had our engagement party, built a house, got married and had our first child. As I look back I don't even know what we were thinking, but I'm glad we had each other every step of the way. The next two years were probably the hardest and darkest times for me during our marriage. I really struggled and looking back I realise I may have been depressed.

To be honest, I don't have the best relationship with my in-laws. I felt I was in a non-stop power struggle for my family with my mother-in-law, who wouldn't let go of her son. She caused constant problems in our marriage, and for a long time, my husband was easily manipulated by her. We would fight all the time; it wasn't a healthy environment for our new son. It got so bad I considered leaving. As a newlywed with a new baby, it should have been the best time of my life, but I was heartbroken on the inside.

My husband had been working as a glazier in Perth, but also had a night job for extra money, so when the opportunity presented for him to get a FIFO job, we thought we had nothing to lose. I secretly hoped it would help our marriage … and it did. In fact, it saved us. He realised how influential his mother had been in our marriage, and vowed to always put us first. He loved having the quality time to spend with us when he was home. He didn't have the best relationship with his father when he was young, so when it comes to our children, he puts in so much effort; they absolutely adore him, and they know how much their dad loves them, every single day.

When my husband first started working away I struggled with solo parenting, the dramas with my in-laws, a second pregnancy and working part-time. I like to think of myself as a strong and independent woman and for the most part I cope pretty well. I'm also very lucky to have a supportive family however, my dad and my brother are also FIFO, my mum works full-time and my sister has two handsome boys of her own. I'm very grateful though, for all the help and company they give me when they can. For a while I struggled to find a support group or collective of women who weren't negative towards the FIFO lifestyle. I wanted to meet others who were making their way through everyday FIFO life. So one night after a few wines, FIFO Wags was born. I had no idea how it would go, but I knew there had to be other women out there feeling the same as me. Now, I love hosting events and great conversation with other FIFO partners. Running this group is one of my greatest achievements and I have met the most amazing women. Nothing makes me happier than seeing women empower, uplift and support each other. There are times I go check out the group after a tough day, and just looking through everyone's posts and stories makes me feel like I'm not alone.

Survival #2: Trust them completely, communicate openly and often.

Last year was a tough year for our family. It started off well and then COVID hit. My eldest son had just started kindy, so now we had to home-school. I had just found out I was pregnant again at the start of the pandemic, and all of sudden we weren't sure what would happen with my hubby's work. He ended up with a roster change from 2:1 to 2:2, which became quite stressful financially. While it was great to have him home for two weeks at a time, especially with home schooling and pregnancy, it also increased our expenses, which hit hard with his loss of income. We also got a case of cabin fever and it felt like our two little boys were often hanging from the light fixtures!

Hubby's roster didn't go back to normal for six months, and during that time when they reopened the playgrounds, my hubby took the boys to play. They were so excited, but whilst on the swings, my youngest son fell off and broke his arm. It was a trip to the local hospital, followed by an ambulance to the children's hospital for late-night emergency surgery. It was an extremely stressful time, made worse by interfering family members. I remember being so exhausted by pregnancy and feeling betrayed, that I just sat at my two-year-old son's bedside all night long, with tears streaming down my face. Over the next couple of months we had regular appointments at the children's hospital to check on his progress, but one day I noticed he was very lethargic and had been sleeping for longer than normal. I knew something was wrong, so I called my mum, who met me at the hospital with my two boys. We were so lucky when we got there, as the surgeon was there doing rounds. He came in, cut off the cast and pulled out the metal rods - and out came all the pus! My son had a bad infection and it was lucky we got him back to the hospital when we did. They reset the arm and gave him antibiotics. He ended up healing well and his arm is fine now.

Survival #3: Be organised. Routine is a must.

While he had his cast on I had to do another dash to emergency, this time on a Saturday night with both boys, because all the bad stuff happens when hubby is away! My eldest son had put something up his nose but I had no idea what it was. We got through ED and it took two nurses and a doctor to get out the foreign object, which actually turned out to be part of my youngest son's cast. Let's just say, he hasn't shoved anything else up his nose since.

Misconception #1: You must be rich.

In between the ED visits I also was going through my third pregnancy. My two previous pregnancies had been high risk, and while at the start this one seemed to be fairly straight-forward, I was full of nerves and always exhausted. I ended up being monitored, as bub had some growth issues. A pregnancy in a pandemic is pretty scary on its own, but throw in FIFO life, two children and emotional stress – well, I was pretty terrified. Thankfully, we were blessed with the safe arrival of our beautiful baby girl in November 2020 and even more blessed to have my husband home for eight weeks while we settled into life as a family of five. It seemed that no matter what curve balls we were thrown, we managed to get through them together.

I often get asked what being a FIFO family is like. FIFO life is definitely hard. It's full of the normal shitty things, like your favourite lipstick being discontinued, COVID lock-downs and your god-awful mother-in-law, but what hits me most, is that things seem to go wrong as soon as your partner walks into the airport. It's the kids that never sleep; the family trips to the ED or the maternity ward on your own; the hot water system shitting itself; the lack of a village; the personal space you never have and the routine specialist you become.

It is also wonderful for the quality family time together you couldn't possibly have with a normal nine-to-five job. It's your husband being there to do the simple things like school pick-up and drop-off, swimming lessons during the day, the last-minute family getaways, brunch dates, the long list of jobs I give him, and having your best friend with you 24/7 for a whole week (even if they do become annoying). While my hubby is away I spend most of my time being a snack bitch, doing school runs, sport runs, and when I can, I go to the gym every day, mostly for my mental health. My gym has the best crèche with the most fabulous ladies, so while I watch Netflix on the treadmill I know my babies are safe. Friends can be your best support network, so I try and catch up with them as much as possible. They are always a good source of advice or a shoulder to cry on. Often one of them has a saucy tale or Tinder conquest to tell, which creates a lot of laughs and no judgement. I'm blessed with a great circle of friends; it really is quality over quantity as you get older.

Misconception #2: The single mother comparisons.

One of the biggest misconceptions of FIFO family life is 'Doesn't your husband miss you? My husband could never be away from us.' Well, of course he misses us, but what man doesn't want to provide the best life possible for his family? My husband works his ass off making sure we have the best of everything. He also loves his job and couldn't possibly do it locally. He really enjoys spending a whole week with his family, indulging in the menial and boring everyday tasks. My husband is very hands-on; he loves changing nappies, reading stories, fixing boo-boos and wiping tears. He does the dishes, mops the floor and gets the food shopping. Whether he is home or away he is constantly supporting his wife, either face-to-face or via FaceTime. He builds me up on a bad day, laughs when I send him tantrum or poo explosion pictures or videos, stays up with sick children and lets me rest, and sends me for a massage or hair appointment when he can see I need a self-care moment. There is a stigma around these hard-working men that all they do is get drunk on site, sleep around or come home and not be a part of the family unit. In my experience, it's just not true, it's a small percentage that give the rest a bad name. The majority of these men are the ultimate family men. Their families mean the world to them.

The connection I share with my husband is amazing, I physically see him one third of the year and in that time we do get physical; the sex is great especially because you only see each other once a month. As soon as he gets into the car at the airport we can feel the spark. It's about making time for each other and catering to each other's needs. It's kind of everywhere and anywhere you can, especially when you have three children. It's also the little things like hugging or hand holding or even just sharing the bed. It's comforting knowing he is there and I'm safe and protected. Communication is key in keeping the romance alive; as are sneaky nudes. He FaceTimes the kids every day and calls me. I send him photo and message updates all day while he is either at work or asleep. When he is home we try and have a date night, whether we go out and enjoy a meal or even just have ice cream and a movie in bed. We are still re-adjusting to having a newborn so we take whatever kind of date night we can.

Misconception #3: That you hate being a FIFO family.

These days our arguments usually revolve around him spending too much time on the lawn or in the toilet and that I spend too much money on children's clothing. If we have a serious argument we are both aware of each other's feelings and know how to make it right. Our number one rule is to never let each other go to bed angry. I am really proud of how far my husband has come professionally, as a father and as a husband. He is an excellent provider, mentor and soul mate. He has now been

FIFO for four-and-a-half years. In the time we have been together he has grown and matured far beyond his years. He is the best husband and father I could ask for. We now have three children, Axl, Ace and Anjel. They are the apples of our eyes, the reason for our grey hairs, the causes of our future heart attacks and our greatest achievements.

In a world full of uncertainty and chaos, having a solid family life is key. FIFO life provides us with a constant routine. While they may only see him through a phone screen, he is never far from their hearts and minds. We have a countdown on our fridge and a daddy doll that gets shared around at bedtime. People seem to forget how amazingly resilient children are. For our children, this is the only life they have known. They think dad works in the paw patrol tower at the airport and nothing beats the joy in their eyes on fly-in day knowing he will be home to tuck them in. To them he is their hero.

'THE FIFO LIFE IS REVEALING - IT REVEALS YOUR STRENGTHS AND YOUR WEAKNESSES. IT PROVIDES YOU WITH AN OPPORTUNITY TO SEARCH WITHIN YOURSELF, WHAT YOU VALUE AND WHAT YOU HOLD OF UTMOST IMPORTANCE IN YOUR RELATIONSHIP AS WELL. MAKE THE MOST OF THE OPPORTUNITIES AND CHALLENGES THAT THE FIFO LIFE (AND LIFE IN GENERAL) THROWS AT YOU - LEARN, EVOLVE, WALLOW IF YOU NEED, THEN GET BACK UP AND KICK BUTT!'

Erica Urquiaga – 'The Technically Not a Wife Wife'

THE TECHNICALLY NOT A WIFE WIFE

NAME: ERICA URQUIAGA
INDUSTRY: MINING OPERATIONS (PROCESS OPERATOR) AND
MINING SERVICES (HUMAN RESOURCES)
RELATIONSHIP STATUS: DE FACTO
TIME IN INDUSTRY: 2012 - 2016 - WORKED FIFO MYSELF,
2016 -2019 WAS THE FIFO 'WIFE' AT HOME WHILE MY PARTNER
CONTINUED TO WORK AWAY. CONTINUE TO BE INVOLVED IN THE
MINING INDUSTRY IN A HUMAN RESOURCES CAPACITY

This is a short snippet of my FIFO journey and the lessons I learned. There are a lot more stories, ups, downs and everything in between that comes with it but hopefully you enjoy this highlight reel. I continue to tap into this experience for strength, life lessons and work-related insights.

FIFO, DIDO, rosters, swings: some words you become familiar with very quickly once you or your loved ones venture into the world of working away.

Back in 2012, while I was working in recruitment for a brand-new mining operation in Western Australia, I became intrigued by this whole world of FIFO. Having moved to Perth in 2006, these terms get used a fair bit but I never really thought about doing it myself, until I started recruiting for the new project. My debriefs with hiring managers ended up being more about the plant and I kept asking questions. Finally, one of the superintendents got sick of my cross-examination. When I asked if there was anything someone like me (i.e. inexperienced) could do on-site, he said, 'Yes - an operator.' At this point I wasn't sure what was involved with being an 'operator,' however I did have one very important follow up question – 'Am I going to get dirty?' The answer was a very resounding 'Yes.' And that sealed the deal for me.

At this point my partner was already working on-site and when I told him about the prospect of me going FIFO his response was, 'About bloody time. You keep talking about that plant!' So, a week after my graduation for my masters degree in human resources management, I flew to site.

Survival #1: Mindset and communication are key.

About a month or so before my official start date on-site, I went for a visit to do some recruitment related tasks. While there, the plant superintendent arranged for one of the supervisors to take me for a walk around to see where I'd be working. While walking around the process plant, we started to go up a set of grid mesh stairs. With each step I became slower and slower. The supervisor turned and asked me if I was okay. I said, 'Yes, just a wee bit scared of heights,' to which he scoffed 'Probably want to reconsider your decision to be an operator then.'

And that sort of interaction happened a few times in my first months as an operator. I was scared of heights and there was a lot of working at height. I had a few of the guys ask if I was okay in the head, because they couldn't reconcile that someone working in an office would voluntarily choose to work outside in the elements. Tradition dictates, it's the other way around; you start outside and work your way to the air-conditioning. I was told only idiots do it the other way around.

I ventured into the world of FIFO because I wanted to know what it was about. Working in Perth it's inevitable you'll find yourself involved in mining or oil and gas in some way. It doesn't matter how many degrees of separation, there's bound to be a connection. I didn't want to be working in the corporate office without a deeper understanding of how it actually worked on-site. I had big dreams of becoming a General Manager – Human Resources down the track, and I figured I needed that hands-on experience for added credibility.

For anyone who has worked on-site before, human resources and safety are nobody's favourite. So here I went, fresh from the office, with no muscles or physical strength to speak of, and no idea about pumps, conveyors, screens, wrenches or anything else for that matter. I wasn't someone who dabbled in that area of life, nor am I mechanically inclined. I may not be any of those things, but what I am, is stubborn, curious and eager to learn, which I've learnt from experience, are keys to survival, along with a healthy dose of humour.

It was such a huge move for me that friends requested I start a blog so they could keep up with my adventures and understand what I was up to.

It was October 2012 when I started my first stint on-site. Not only was I the former HR girl from the office, I also had purple boots and a HUGE purple high-vis crib bag. The bag was a present from my partner and I am still not convinced he didn't get it as a big fat joke. It was like walking into a cool school dressed as Steve Urkel! Seriously, all I needed to stand out even more, was a huge sign that said, 'Odd One Out!'

My partner, Martin, had already been working on-site, but I wanted to experience it on my terms, so we had separate rooms. Seriously, after a strenuous twelve-hour day being out and about in the elements, there was no way I was going to be good company. However, he worked in a completely different part of the operation. He was in the office, and I was out in the plant getting grubby in the heat, rain and whatever Mother Nature chucked at us.

The early days were challenging. The transition from office to mine site, (not an operational one at that point but in the final stages of construction), was filled with all sorts of new rules and things to look out for. I was scared to walk around the plant on my own for the first couple of swings, for fear of breaking the rules; walking too close to mobile plant in operation or going under a suspended load by mistake. What was second nature to these guys was so foreign to me.

I even struggled with 'old mate.' As a migrant who is not proficient in Aussie slang, I first thought 'old mate' was a specific person. I spent close to three swings trying to figure out who old mate was. I was also told that the franna (crane) was a franger. I didn't know what a franger was, so I proceeded to refer to the franna as that for some time before I was corrected.

When I started, I was the only girl in a crew of sixteen. I had to show them that I was serious about being an operator. I had to prove myself worthy of the spot. I went through the paces and slowly they realised I was serious, and wasn't just out for a two-month stint before running back to the comforts of an air-conditioned office.

Credit to my crew though, most of them were really good at teaching me and guiding me through the ropes. Even with my fear of heights, as long as I tried, I had their support. Some of the females on other crews couldn't even get on the tools. Some of the older crew would swoop in and take the wrench from their hands, and literally sideline them. An older guy from the other crew, (I want to write gentleman but seriously, it wasn't gentlemanly behaviour), once told me during handover day that he didn't have a problem with females being on the crew, he just didn't think they should be there as it wasn't a job for a female. Make sense of that! This was the same guy that would ask the female in his crew to do the menial running around, while he did the actual job, so there was no opportunity to learn or improve.

Initially and naïvely, I thought that the 'proving myself and learning the ropes' bit was going to be the key challenge. Sadly, I was wrong. Oh so very wrong. Once I actually learned the ropes and could do the job, that was when the resentment started; the vibe started changing – for the worse.

Survival #2: Thick skin and stubbornness may help (helped me heaps anyway).

Not only did I have to deal with the physical and technical learning curve, as well as the being-scared-of-heights-thing while working in the plant, I also knew there were rumours going around about me. Before I even started on-site, my partner had told me there were rumours that I was sleeping with three guys in the office. It was swirling all around site. News to me, as none of it was true. By the time I got to site, the rumour was that I was sleeping with the superintendent, which is how I got the gig in the first place. When I managed to keep the job, the story then became it was because I was sleeping with my supervisor.

I went into mining with the mindset that I was going to learn what it was like from the ground up. I knew it wasn't going to be easy being female in a male-dominated industry. The way I approached it was this: if I were to join a basketball team, I would have to learn the rules, the ins and outs, understand the culture and everything else that came with being part of the team. I wasn't going to go in and demand things be changed to suit me. For instance, there were no female toilets in a certain area I was working in. This was understandable as I was the only female in that area, and I didn't see it as adding value to ask for a female toilet if I was the only one who needed it. I learnt to check who was in there and managed to co-exist with everyone else. I didn't want to demand changes; I wanted to understand why things were the way they were.

Thankfully, six months into my stint on-site, I was lucky enough to have another female join the crew. This absolute legend had fifteen years of mining experience under her belt, and along with another late addition to the crew (a dude), they made my experience better. Miss Sammy came first. Before she started (unbeknownst to me), most of my crew had bets going as to how long it would last before I claimed my territory – their words, not mine. According to them, having two females on one crew was never going to work. Apparently, being there first, I was going to lay my claim on 'my boys' (again, their words) and it was going to be tense.

Survival #3: Ask for help.

Unfortunately for the lads, they never got the girl fight they anticipated. We got on really well, and still do to this day. Instead of a cat-fight, the crew had to put up with us cackling and laughing our heads off. They were fairly disappointed, and I'm not sure if it was because I wasn't keen to claim them as 'my boys,' or that they now had two capable females helping each other through it all.

A few months later came Mike. It bothered the crew that we got along so well, and he didn't want to mingle too much with them. Mike taught me that not all guys are the same. He also taught me the art of drinking tea. When I had the sniffles, I would come back from my checks with a tea waiting for me in the crib room. This was unusual for the boys, some of whom asked my partner if it bothered him that I was getting on so well with a guy. For the record, it did not bother my legend of a partner.

The more comfortable and confident I got with the technical and physical aspect of the job, the worse the rumours became and the resentment increased. One night, in a split second slip, I ended up with an injured swollen wrist and no one could figure out what was actually wrong with it. That was the beginning of eighteen months of intense 'character building'. I struggle to label it bullying because I fought back initially, but it just become exhausting. I gave it back as hard as I copped it, but didn't realise what the actual effects were until months later.

When I hurt my wrist, I was taken off the field and put into an office doing other tasks. Having been office-based before going into the great outdoors, I was quick in getting things done and constantly looking for more to do. I tried to make the most of that situation, by being productive and delivering, which unfortunately led to even more resentment. Because, apparently, if you are injured and trying to lift your spirits by smiling and making the most of a crappy situation, that meant you were milking the situation and 'faking' an injury. I took that on the chin for nearly two years. However, the moment of truth came when I was trying to add more value to a job I was given, but instead I was told not to think. Thinking was not my job.

The chance of me winning the lotto is a lot higher than the chances of me switching off to improvement opportunities!

The wrist injury led to the end of my illustrious manual labour career, and I transitioned into being the home-based half of a FIFO relationship.

The biggest learning for me is how important mindset is when working away. The ability to flip a not-so-good situation, and be able to see the advantages you can take from it, makes such a big difference. As much as we like to think the industry is ready for increased female participation, the reality is that there are some people who do not share that view. Any female going into mining needs to understand that historically it's a male-dominated industry. Although there are massive calls now for increased numbers of women, and the ever-controversial quotas, you need to go in with an open mind; learn the rules (the official and unofficial ones), before trying to go in and change them. You need to have thick skin to survive, but then again, that goes for everyone, regardless of gender. At the end of the day, the biggest lesson for me is that it's all in how I frame my experience. Mindset is key. Having allies really helps through the crappiest of days, but most of all, ask for help when the going gets tough.

When things got hard, I would focus on the advantages of working on-site; being away from the temptation of the KFC empire, and not having to think about what to cook and only worry about laundry and waking up on time. I loved the magical sunsets and sunrises, the full moon on night shift. There are many wonderful things that you get to see and experience when you work on a remote site. I made a point to appreciate all of these things. Even with three years of flying in and out on the same route, I made sure to look outside the window each time and appreciate the unique landscape. Looking at things with wonder and gratitude shifts so much. It's way better than being in that 'not this crap again' frame of mind. It doesn't help you or the people around if you exude negativity.

Misconception #1: Females will struggle – everyone struggles, and everyone needs thick skin regardless of gender.

Females have a different set of strengths and we must recognise this. We had a crew member pass away overnight at camp. It was a harrowing experience for all. However, when it came time for his wife and daughters to come to site, I really wanted to be the one to speak on behalf of the crew. The crew were okay with it, as none of them knew what to do in that situation. I went on to meet the family at camp and told them how valued their husband and dad was. One of the boys (who would later become my biggest tormentor), came with me and on our way back to site, gave me a hug. He was baffled at how I managed to connect with the family. But it was just something I knew how to do. When it came to the funeral, the family asked me to speak on behalf of the crew. It was two months after I delivered a eulogy for my own father's funeral. As I was re-telling a story of when the deceased had dropped the dreaded 'C' word accidentally on the radio one night shift, I could see the worried faces of my crew, they genuinely thought I was going to say the word in front of everyone at the funeral. I didn't. I chose to say Carrot instead, (hey, it starts with C and ends with T, close enough) and had the whole room in stitches. Most of us females may not be as physically strong as some of the guys, but don't ever forget that we are strong in other ways.

If you are grumpy, frustrated, or annoyed, it will be dismissed as the time of the month, 90% of the time. If I had a penny for every time I copped this, I would be retired by now. The number of times I had to explain, 'No, it's not that time of the month, this just doesn't make sense and that's why I'm reacting this way.' Or the classic, 'No, it's not that time of the month, you are just being an idiot hence the current situation we are in.' But that never worked; they knew my cycle better than me. You learn to pick your battles after some time!

Another hot tip, if you are looking to work on-site, leave your bathroom door open overnight, especially in winter. Why, you ask? When living in a donga, approximately 3x3 metres, the aircon regulates the whole space. If you leave your bathroom door open and you have your room at a certain temperature, the bathroom temp is the same as your room. If you leave your bathroom door closed, you may have your room at twenty-six degrees, but when you open your bathroom, you are slapped in the face by a very fresh four degrees. I used to set my alarm at 3 am, change the room temperature to thirty degrees, have my peanut butter sandwich while still half asleep, and by 3.30 am I was out of my room and headed to the gym.

> **Misconception #2: It's good money or everyone is in it for the money- break it down to an hourly rate and the sacrifices that come with it, there's a reason why the pay is that way. Being in it solely for the money doesn't make it easier.**

Although I had my own challenges while working on-site, I also got to witness the challenges everyone else faced.

Dedicated family men away from their families, unable to help their partners with the household responsibilities, missing out on children's milestone because they worked away. It was really hard seeing the guys when they were particularly down about missing family. There's not much you can do to help them, except listen to the stories and engage.

Another common theme were the blokes who really didn't want to do FIFO but had partners who didn't want to work. They had to be the sole earners and felt they couldn't afford to work a city-based nine-to-five job. There were people with knee and back aches, who had to trudge up and down stairs several times a day just because they were the sole earners.

Some partners would send the guys photos of them out and

about shopping, while they were on-site, slugging it out, sometimes hating every minute of it. Other partners think that site is like a little holiday outing where you get to hang out the bar at the end of the day. It's not a party, and when you go to the bar, you are there with the same people you have spent the day with; some are people you may not want to hang out with in the real world, but on-site, you don't have much of a choice.

It's not all bad, but it's also not all good all the time; definitely not a holiday! When you want to get away, have a change of scenery or eat something different to what's on the menu – you can't. Hence, the importance of being able to flip that mindset.

When I first transitioned to being the at-home partner, I wasn't in the best mindset. The challenges of the previous eighteen months finally came to a head. I had internalised so much, I was couchbound for several months. I wasn't ready to go back to being in an environment with other people. It took some time to realise and process through the scars. A panic attack while out in public, when I thought I saw one of the boys, made me realise I had work to do to process the experience.

I started my own business because I wasn't ready to face being part of the workforce yet. I needed time to process all the crap I experienced and deal with it properly.

Being the at-home one had its perks; I had my own space. When my partner came home was when the stepdaughters came home too. When he was on-site I was by myself – sounds awesome right? Unless you are a wuss who can't completely relax because there's a noise outside at 1 am. I used to message him about car alarms going off at 3 am or the fire alarm going mental at 5 am and not knowing what to do. I used to sleep during the day because at night, I couldn't sleep and did not feel safe.

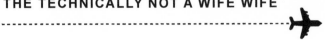

Basically when you are the partner at home, you are on a FIFO schedule too. I didn't have to manage kids (I take my hat off to those who do that on their own), but I had my own routine and way of going about my week.

When my partner came home, he changed the way things were. He basically just barged in and did things his way. In his head, I am sure he was not barging in, he was just doing things the way he thought it should be done. But boy, did that do my head in! Some weeks, I lashed out because it annoyed me so much. Other weeks (probably didn't happen as often as I thought), I would let it go. After all, he had just come back from being on-site, you don't have the same freedom as you do when you get home. More than likely, he also wasn't having the time of his life while on-site, and just wanted to do things his way when he got home.

Overall, in my experience, there are negatives and positives in either scenario. Neither is a walk in the park. Neither is easy. But both come with certain sets of freedoms; FIFO means being home for a longer amount of time, unlike just weekends or nights if you work the standard nine-to-five. In both situations, mindset and communication are the keys to thriving. Each situation is unique, as each relationship is unique, however, both partners need to understand that it's not necessarily easier on the other side. Being part of the FIFO workforce is a choice we make, and comes with compromises. There's no one hot tip to make the experience better for anyone. There are things that I did to make my experience a positive one for me; if not positive, one that I could learn from, at the very least. Understanding your partner also has bad days or weeks with their own set of challenges, is a good starting point. It's not helpful to think that the other has it better than us because they are the ones who get to go away or get to stay home.

FIFO is not easy, but then nothing in life is. It's a decision and a choice that is made, and the consequences need to be managed. Whatever the reason you decide to take on the FIFO life, remember you have made that choice and to think of the goal. It's a journey; some days will be harder than others – for both parties. The important thing is mindset, communication and support. When the going gets tough, talk it through and reset as needed. Keep the end goal in mind, but also, sometimes it's okay to wallow in a bad day. We are human beings; complex, emotional creatures, and we are allowed to have bad days. Just don't let the bad days snowball into an unmanageable beast. Ask for help when you need it. Just because your partner isn't physically there, doesn't mean you are alone.

> Misconception #3: People sleep around at camp – not the case for most. Not saying it doesn't happen but definitely there is such a thing as platonic relationships even on a mine site!

All FIFO journeys are different but hopefully in sharing mine, you can tap into your own experience to explore how strong you really are. Pat yourself on the back for every win! Use the learning opportunities/challenges as character building exercises.

'ALWAYS TRUST YOUR GUT FEELINGS. SOMETIMES WHEN IT'S TOO GOOD TO BE TRUE, IT USUALLY IS. MAINTAIN HOPE, BUT DON'T BE NAÏVE. IT TRULY IS A MAN'S WORLD AND UNFORTUNATELY, WE ARE JUST VISITORS WITH A TEMPORARY VISA. THEY MAY BE STRONGER THAN US BUT THEY WILL NEVER BE SMARTER THAN US. WE ARE WIRED DIFFERENTLY AND I HAVE ACCEPTED THAT.
GOD, MEN ARE SUCH PIGS.'

Anon – 'The Secret Wife'

THE SECRET WIFE

NAME: ANON
INDUSTRY: GOLD MINING
RELATIONSHIP STATUS: SINGLE & READY TO MINGLE
TIME IN INDUSTRY: 4 YEARS TOO LONG

I left my hometown when I was fifteen as my mum said I could get a better education in Australia; Queensland to be precise. My aunty Annie and her Aussie husband took me in. I was promised sunshine, ample career opportunities and a loving home. I'll save you the guessing game, everything went opposite to my idealistic dreams.

> Survival #1: Get a friend with some batteries. Those lonely nights hit different.

Let me start at the beginning. My aunty was a doting wife. By definition, she was a slave. There was never any physical abuse but with her small-minded village mentality, she thought being a servant was normal. I hated living there. My overweight uncle would constantly make passes at me. I couldn't bear to tell my aunty as she has done so much for me. She tried for years, but couldn't have kids and she felt guilty she wasn't able to provide him with children, so she encouraged my uncle and I to get close, to bond like father and daughter. Nothing eventuated from his passes until I hit eighteen and he was drunk. He came into my room one night smelling of alcohol and dripping in sweat. He crawled up onto my bed and started kissing my face. I don't believe in God anymore but I thank God my aunty woke up that night to go the toilet. That startled him enough to leave my room. God, men are such pigs.

Survival #2: Start a hobby or join a group.

The next morning I ran away to Jessica's house, a lady I had met at church. She could only house me for two weeks as she was heading off to work in the mines. I asked her what the mines were and she laughed at me. She said, 'Sweetie, it's where people go to get rich.' I was sold, if I had my own money I wouldn't need to go back to my aunty's house. At that moment, God if you like, Jessica received a text from her supervisor saying one of her colleagues had quit and they were looking for more employees. Within twenty-four hours I was on-site. It was so red, so much dirt, hot and flooded with flies. I scored a job as a cleaner. That job worked for me because I struggled with English. I had only been in Australia for three years by this time. We only spoke Filipino at home and I wasn't allowed to mingle with anyone else out of school.

I felt uncomfortable on-site. Like a piece of meat surrounded by hungry lions. They whistled at me, made sex gestures with their hands and yelled things like, 'How much?' I started to get flashbacks of my uncle and his disgusting ways. God, men are such pigs. I was alone, once again in another foreign place. My friend was on a different site and there weren't many women on this site. I felt very unsafe. I worked, went to the mess, got my food and ate in my room. I would prop a chair up against the door, so no one could come in during the night.

In my second week, I was making a bed and there was a $50 note under the pillow. I didn't think anything about it until I went to the next room and there was another $50 note under the pillow. I thought that this was a test; that everyone was against me and trying to get me fired. Like the other room, I put the note on the bedside table. At least twelve other beds had the same $50 note pattern. I asked my male supervisor if he knew what that was about. He was an Indian guy and I don't know if it was his accent that threw me, but I heard 'tip tip.' I found out later he said 'jig jig' (a word used instead of 'sex,' common in Asian countries). Here I am thinking, oh maybe I have badly judged these guys and they aren't that bad. The next day I started pocketing the notes. This time there was only six. Two nights later, I got a knock on my door. There was an Aussie guy, beer in hand, belly popping out of his top. He said, 'I'm here to claim my prize.' I said, 'Sorry I no understand.' He banged his fist against my wall and said, 'I pay you for sex.' My heart sunk. It all made sense now. I quickly ran to get his money, but he barged into my room. Another worker Dave walked past and noticed him being aggressive. He asked if everything was okay and I just ran out the room. Dave followed me and consoled me as I cried.

> **Survival #3: SAVE. And save some more. Have your own secret stash of money for when shit hits the fan. A little trick I learnt from Ginger (Sharon Stone) in the movie Casino - love doesn't mean stuff all when he hates you.**

Dave made me feel safe. He made me feel comfortable. I had never had a boyfriend before. My dad died when I was young so I never felt respectful love from a man before. Our relationship developed quickly and effortlessly. He moved me out of camp and helped me start a business in the town, twenty minutes from site and a couple hours from Perth. We lived together when he was working on this site, and alternated with a site in Sydney. Six months later, I found out I was pregnant. I was so happy. He too was happy to have his first child. I couldn't believe how perfect my life was going. That was until he left his iPad at home for one swing. I was cooking dinner and wanted to look up a recipe online. My phone was charging, so I grabbed the iPad and turned it on. An influx of texts came in from a lady named 'Love of my life.' My heart dropped. There were hundreds and hundreds of text exchanges, photos, emails, you name it. Turns out he was married with kids. His swing in Sydney was where his family lived. He had three boys, the oldest was sixteen. I tried to call him, but his phone was off. Oh yeah, turns out he had two phones, which I found out later.

> Misconception #1: 'I bet she's sleeping with the neighbour.' This is getting old. Thank you, next.

When he finally checked in on me, I confronted him about what I saw. He cowardly told me he is ending it with her, she's evil and he wants to be with me. I believed him. God, men are such pigs. I asked him if she knew about me and he said no, because he didn't want her to take all his money in the divorce. He wanted our daughter to have the money. I was trapped, again. He had done so much for me I couldn't leave him, where would I go? I was pregnant and had no friends or family to turn to. I gave birth to my daughter with him by my side. The nurse took some snaps on that infamous iPad. We posed. I forced a smile and he was beaming with joy from finally having a little girl. Then, guess what? That iPad was synced to his Sydney family's iCloud account and his wife found the photos. Within half an hour of giving birth, she was calling him on Facebook (because his Sydney phone was switched off). He panicked thinking there was something wrong with his boys, so he caved and answered after her thirty-seventh attempt at calling. As he was holding our new daughter, he was grovelling like a little bitch to his wife denying everything she was asking him.

Now, she must have enjoyed the FIFO lifestyle, because this bitch stayed too. How dumb are we? We both accepted the fact that he had two separate families on opposite sides of Australia because we were bound by his money and pathetic promises. I went on to have two more kids and one miscarriage. She also had more kids, twins in fact. So much for getting a divorce, hey! Then this guy who was sashaying like a king, got promoted to a really high position. That meant his pay cheque went up. He started to change. He stopped making an effort, he didn't attend school events for the kids and he didn't even want to have sex. He would openly chat to me, or his wife, in each other's company and he even took my kids to Sydney to meet the family. When he took them without asking my permission, I knew I needed a way out. I started to create fraudulent invoices for my business, which he was still funding from his FIFO pay cheque. From these fake invoices and my weekly allowance, I managed to secretly save $200,000 in two years. I knew I wanted to leave him, I just didn't know when or how. The FIFO lifestyle worked for me as I didn't have to see him for half of the year.

> Misconception #2: 'You're so lucky you get to be a stay at home wife.' Uh ok, the house and kids maintain themselves do they?

I ended up befriending another Filipina lady, Rosalie, who I met at the hairdresser. Turns out, her partner worked on the same site as my children's father. She had also moved to Australia when she was a teenager. We bonded and had a great friendship. She worked as a cook, on a 3:1 rotation. On her time off we would go to cafes, the salon and the swimming pool. We never went to each other's houses because we already felt trapped at home and wanted a change of scene. She didn't have any family or friends either, but really enjoyed the flexibility of the FIFO lifestyle. One day as we sipped our cappuccinos, she couldn't stop smiling. I said in Filipino, 'What's wrong with you mahal you going to share?' She flashed a ring on her left hand and squealed, 'I'm getting married!' I had so much hate towards men, not once in our friendship did I ever ask to see what her fiancé looked like. And well, she knew I hated my partner so she didn't bother either. We both weren't active on social media as our partners frowned upon it. However I was so happy for my friend, I asked to see a picture of her and her fiancé. She giggled and handed me the phone. My jaw dropped! It was Dave. He was at it again. She was me, just a newer model. And you know what, I didn't even feel sad. In fact, I laughed hysterically. My friend though, didn't find it quite as funny as me … obviously.

> **Misconception #3: 'You guys must be so rich? I'm jealous.' You know we pay up to 40% tax right?**

When Dave came home that night, to my house, Rosalie made a guest appearance. He was sprung. Turns out he had been hooking up with multiple women on-site as his families stupidly waited for him to return from his shift.

Yes, men cheat. But it's not just on-site. If they want to have sex with someone else, they will during their on or off swing. I say trust your gut and if it doesn't feel right, it's probably not. As for me, I left him and am now living back in Queensland with my children, financially independent. He sees them once a year, his preference. Rosalie left him and the site she worked on immediately. As for his wife, well, she is still living her best life, not lifting a finger, because daddy's pay cheque covers her housekeeper, her bills, her nails, her hair, her new breasts, her car and everything else she wants. Too bad he can't pay for some common decency, hey. God, men are such pigs.

'YOU CAN ENTER BROKE AND LEAVE RICH (OR NOT). PERHAPS YOU KNOW NO ONE ON ARRIVAL AND LEAVE WITH FOREVER MATES. WHEN YOU JOIN THE INDUSTRY THE POSSIBILITIES ARE ENDLESS. WILL YOU TAKE A CHANCE? IF YOU ARE UP FOR A CAREER AND LIFE CHALLENGE, CHOOSE FIFO!'

Brenda Denbesten – 'The Engineering Wife'

THE ENGINEERING WIFE

NAME: BRENDA DENBESTEN
INDUSTRY: COPPER, GOLD, URANIUM
RELATIONSHIP STATUS: MARRIED
TIME IN INDUSTRY: 15 YEARS

As an 18-year-old, my friends all seemed to know what they wanted to do at university and I had no idea. I didn't want to be a doctor or lawyer, which are the first preferences for African parents. One of the girls in my chemistry and physics class told me she was going to be a chemical engineer. 'What do they do?' I asked. She said they run factories and make products. Immediately, my mind thought of L'Oreal and the jingle from their adverts, 'L'Oreal, because you're worth it.' I was sold. I wanted to be one too. I put the plan into motion, packed my bags and left Zimbabwe, my parents and all that I'd known, to study chemical engineering.

When I finished my degree, there were no open roles with cosmetic companies, and I had to act fast. I decided to try mining. There was something really cool about turning dirt into gold. So I decided to continue building my career in the mining industry.

As I exited the small fifty-seat aeroplane, I was greeted with a gust of hot wind and a swarm of flies. My first thought 'What have I done?'

I was a vibrant, single, twenty-seven-year-old, chemical engineer when I made a bold decision. I moved from the bright city lights of Sydney to a small, dusty town in South Australia called Roxby Downs; from a city with millions of people, to a town with a population of 5000. Was I scared? Heck yes! But the possibility of crafting a career that I enjoyed and loved was greater than the fear.

> **Survival #1: Give the experience a chance. Ask questions, make meaningful connections as you build your career. You don't have to go on this journey alone, you are guaranteed to make some lifetime friends.**

So many questions had run through my mind. Will there be shopping? (I mean come on; this is an important consideration, right?) Would there be other black people there? Would I last or would I regret it? These questions were answered in the first fifteen minutes as we completed the tour of the town. To understand what this remote town was like, picture this; one small shopping centre which had one supermarket, one butcher, a mixed take-away/café, a gift shop, a surf shop and ... that's it ...! Did your heart just sink? Mine certainly did! There was a sports centre containing a gym, volleyball courts and netball courts, which doubled up as indoor cricket courts and basketball courts. I'm not sure if you could call a car wash and laundromat a 'shop,' but the guys enjoyed frequenting this, and the Mitre 10 for home renovation and car supplies.

Oh, this is Australia, so of course there were two pubs. And last but not least, the 'village camps' that I would soon call home.

I remember laying down that night thinking, 'What the heck have I done?' The small drab room that was assigned to me is called a 'donga.' Essentially, it's a 6x4 metre ensuite room. There was a single bed, covered with an over-washed drab quilt cover, a flat pillow and scratchy sheets. (Note to self: order a pillow online ASAP). Oh, I should mention the old brown leather chair, which sat in the corner and had probably absorbed plenty of sweat from burly men. You can guess ... I hardly sat in that chair!

There was also a small TV, on which I was lucky to get four or five channels, which weren't the ABC News, and a small sliding door that opened up into the bathroom. And that was it. The place I was now to call 'home.'

After a few days, my mind shifted slightly, maybe this wasn't so bad. I walked back into my room after work and found my bed was made for me. There was a cleaning service that came around to empty the bins, and change the sheets and towels twice a week. That made me smile, I could get used to this.

Another bonus when you move, many companies offer relocation benefits as an incentive. I was able to get my car relocated, and a team of people came to my house and packed up all my stuff. It arrived a couple of weeks later. I thought that was really cool, because who in their right mind likes moving? I had been given a residential position, but they promised it would be FIFO within six months. There was also a waiting list for company housing, so we all had to do some time in the camp village.

> **Survival #2: Be intentional about having open channels of communication. Try and talk to your loved ones at least once a day. I know this is a common challenge on many sites, especially when working underground where there can be no mobile network.**

Because everyone in the town had come from another city themselves, everyone was in a situation where they knew nobody and missed the bustle of a city life. This meant I could connect on common ground with those that started the same year as me. I, as an engineer, didn't actually go there for the graduate program, but there were lots of graduates who started the same year, so I found it quite easy to gel with them and create bonds in my new social circle. We had lots of fun playing table tennis in the recreational room, having barbecues, plus having a drink whenever we could, to dull away the pain. I remember one weekend after I found out I was moving to a FIFO roster; eight days on and six days off. We went out to the pub. I called my friends to the bar and shouted 'FIFO, bitches!!' and bought a few rounds of tequila shots. Those were the good days!

> Survival #3: The perks certainly outweigh the downsides. Working for half a year is a gig anyone would want to secure. The money can really help clear debt and establish a firm foundation. There is so much opportunity. It is a great place for young families depending on the location.

Perhaps it is time to get real. Nothing prepares you for the heat. Fifty-degree days in summer literally feel like the sun is a metre or so above you. In the winter, it gets below zero - another fun desert fact. No one talks about loneliness. No one talks about the isolation and how to maintain your mental health. I was working twelve hours a day; waking up early, going to the mess (dining room) for breakfast and packing a meal for lunch. You then make sure you don't miss the bus, get to work and change into your mine clothes. The day starts with a handover meeting, and getting on with the activities for the day. Once the clock strikes, and the work is suitably complete, you can shower, get changed back into your clothes, wait for the bus and go back to camp. Maybe you want to go have a cold beer, exercise, talk to some friends and decompress. Perhaps the food is unpalatable tonight and you make a quick trip to the supermarket for noodles and tuna. After this you get to your room and you're tired; you just want to close your eyes because in a few short hours you have to do it all again. It's literally that monotonous.

With the boredom and isolation, I drank more alcohol than I needed to, particularly on weekends. Friday night was 'the Club' night and Saturday was 'the Tavern' night, or if you preferred a blend, pick your pub. Maybe, if someone had a house and a pool, we would go to a pool party. You had to be careful about getting too drunk because then the rumours would fly around like wildfire. I avoided being part of the gossip chain as much as possible.

I found as a single girl in the middle of nowhere, surrounded by hundreds, or even thousands of men, it was still very hard to find someone worthy of beginning a relationship with. It was three years in that town before anything exciting happened. At that stage, I wasn't really in the mood for men as I had recently come out of a very toxic relationship in Sydney, which left me with a six week stint in a maximum security female prison! (Now that is a chapter for another book, but let's just say I had some trust issues.) But it happened. Fifteen months before I left that town, I met my now husband. It was a Saturday night at 'the Tavern' pub, and he was cranking out some cool dance moves. I thought to myself, 'Who is this white boy? I am picking up what you are throwing down!'

> **Misconception #1: 'Don't you worry about your husband cheating and being seduced?'** There are plenty of horror stories you hear from people in the industry. My view at the end of the day is your husband can be seduced anywhere. So, manage what is in your control, communicate regularly and be open if any concerns arise.

We had a lovely dance for the rest of the night. He walked me to my house, and he asked me if I would go for breakfast the following morning. Nobody has ever asked me out for breakfast before, and I thought, oh, that was such a gentlemanly thing to do. So, I gave him the benefit of the doubt. Sure enough, the next morning he came over and picked me up for my breakfast date!

If you were to ask him how we met, he would tell you it was actually a couple of weeks before this. I had gone to the sports centre to give mixed indoor soccer a try. Sure enough, he was the tall soccer pro who was trying to give me tips on how to play better. Little did I know he already had an eye on me, leading up to the Dutch courage he displayed on the dance floor. And I suppose the rest is history. We have been married for five years now, which is cool.

> Misconception #2: 'My husband could never be away for that long.' This presumes that your husband prefers to be away for work than home with the family. This is very far from the truth, and is harder on him being away from us.

I am no longer living a FIFO lifestyle, but my husband is. We moved to Melbourne, and he does a week on, week off with day shift and night shift. Being on the other side and waiting until that FIFO period commences, I found that I have had to just get into a routine. I get my son ready, I drop him off at day care, I go to work, I make dinner, pick him up, get him fed, get him bathed, read a book, and bedtime. And I repeat and fill those moments of void with something that edifies me. I love personal development; I can mix up reading a book or listening to a podcast. COVID opened up a whole bunch of things on the internet. For example, I can now join a webinar, start a course, go on to Skillshare and learn a new skill or hobby. So I've found that I can actually fill time quite well. And of course, contact loved ones by sending messages, getting on the phone and talking to hubby every day. My husband appreciates me holding down the fort while he is away. He loves having the time with his son. When he is home, he makes dinner and puts him to bed every night because I get to do it when he's not home. He helps with the laundry, he washes dishes. He actually gets the mop out a whole lot more to get the floorboards gleaming ... I know, is there more where he came from?

> **Misconception #3: 'You must be loaded with cash.'** Yes I should be, but am I? They say money should be like a thermometer not a thermostat; one measures the rise and the other adjusts to the normal target. The more you earn, the more you spend, until the money is back to 'normal.' So set proper financial goals!

COVID was hard in 2020, because Melbourne had an extended lockdown which ended up being for nine months. I did not see him, as the borders were shut for the whole duration. He went for twelve weeks, then ten weeks and then six weeks, coming back for just a couple of weeks in between. As I write this, Melbourne has just been thrown into another lockdown. So we take things as they come. I use my routines to get back into the swing of things. I focus on what I can control, not what I can't control, and that's how we hold everything together in our household.

What would I change?

- I really didn't like coming home after a long, hard day to that 6x4 lifeless room. My dream is to have a service where camp rooms can be modified to themes that may suit your palate and help you relax when you get home. Think Scandi or Boho chic, perhaps coastal or modern. These would give you a sense of coming home, because that was very far from the red desert sands that surrounded that little town.

- Village life has a lot of scope for improvement. Look, I wasn't paying for the meals or accommodation, but it doesn't make it easier when there's hardly any palatable selections in the dining area (also known as the mess).

The small microwave in the donga came in handy to try and make plan B when the food that was served at camp was inedible. My husband still jokes that three out of four times, the meals are slop. I was grateful, nevertheless.

- I have so many good friends that I'm still in touch with today; lifelong friends who understand what it was like to put our life on pause somewhat, because to be honest, it was hard. When I remember my FIFO lifestyle, I'm reminded that it's like you are stuck between two worlds. When I moved to Sydney, I thought it would be cool, but in the six days I was off, most of my friends would be working, for at least five of them. There's no time to call those friends you haven't really hung out with for the last three months while at work, because you are so busy. People didn't have the time to come and relax with me, which meant it could be quite lonely during the time off. (Shopping malls helped!)

- The salaries for FIFO workers are high. However, although I had plenty of money to splash, I found I was actually in debt. New clothes, going out and international travel were so appealing! Credit cards flowed and I spent more than I earned. I was not intentional about savings or investment. I didn't have much to show for it. If I were to do it all over again, stocks, super, and property would be things I would invest in while completing my FIFO stint.

I hope you have enjoyed knowing a little bit about my experience with the FIFO lifestyle. If you are asking whether FIFO is for you, I say, 'YES, go for it. You only live once!'

'WE ALL HAVE DIFFERENT LEVELS OF DESIRES, IT'S UP TO YOU TO DECIDE WHAT YOU'RE WILLING TO ACCEPT. IF THERE IS A VOID IN YOUR RELATIONSHIP, YOU WILL START LOOKING FOR ALTERNATIVE PLACES TO FILL THAT VOID. BUT REMEMBER, CUT OUT THE OUTSIDE NOISE, WHATEVER ARRANGEMENT WORKS FOR YOU GUYS IS NO ONE ELSE'S BUSINESS.'

Anon – 'The Porn Star Wife'

THE PORN STAR WIFE

NAME: ANON
INDUSTRY: OIL & GAS
RELATIONSHIP STATUS: MARRIED
TIME IN INDUSTRY: 9 YEARS

I f you had asked me when I was fifteen how I saw my life by
the time I reached thirty, I would have given some real day-
dreamy doleful answer; something about taking long walks on
the beach with my high school sweetheart, Pete.

Although I did marry my high school sweetheart, and we are
still together now, those long walks on the beach turned into long
talks - otherwise known as arguments, due to his porn addiction.
I'm not naïve to think that he didn't enjoy some X-rated movies
before his lonely FIFO lifestyle, but I can confirm that weeks away
with just his hand, some lube and stacks of tissues, only led to
amplify his addiction.

Survival #1: Keep the sex life passionate when he is home and
when he is away. Send pics, send videos heck even do a little
cheeky facetime action.

Please, amuse me for a paragraph whilst I set the scene. In
year ten, my dad got a job in a new state, so I was transferred to
a new school in suburban Melbourne. This school was massive

and a far cry from the small private all-girls school I had been attending in Sydney. With my nose stuck in my diary trying to figure out where the classroom for science with Mr. Davies was, I took the corner too fast and yep you guessed it, I bumped into Pete. Unbeknownst to us, that run-in would be the start of our bumpy forever. We went to house parties and made out all night. We ditched school and dry humped in the park. That progressed to base two, where our hands would go exploring below the belt.

> **Survival #2: Have a backup plan. The FIFO lifestyle won't last forever.**

My parents were prudes; I had never seen them hold hands, let alone give a peck on the cheek. Having sex, unmarried, in high school was a thought that never crossed my mind. Until Mr. Romantic proposed he should take my V-card after our year eleven Formal. I was so in love with him, so if that's what I needed to do to keep him happy, hey, I was up for it. There was a dedicated banging room set up at Simon's house after party. The room had a lamp draped with red material, a bowl of condoms and a stack of towels. We all waited in a line, like we were lining up to an all-exclusive event. There was a handwritten note on the door with a list of rules. Basically saying 'put a towel down because I don't want virgin blood on my bed.' It was our turn. We did it. It didn't last very long but it hurt like hell. I didn't enjoy it one bit and it was awkward as hell.

We got married at nineteen. I couldn't see a future without him and he felt the same. Our life was text book perfect. No fights. No drama. Good sex (mostly missionary but good sex, I thought). Hubby landed a job straight out of uni as an engineer on a 3:3 roster. That was my man. I was so proud of him, so excited for him to continue succeeding. It never occurred to me how lonely, depressing and challenging this new chapter was going to be. I had spent every single day with this man since I was fifteen, and now I'm told I have to spend three weeks away from him. The reality didn't kick in until I didn't hear from him for four days, as the site was struggling for reception. My stomach was churning. I was creating unrealistic stories in my head. He finally rang and I snapped. We had our first fight. I don't know what came over me. I missed him; like really missed him and the first thing I say is, 'Finally you make contact. What the hell were you thinking?' Of course, I instantly regretted it, but it was impulsive. And his response broke my heart even more. 'Wow babe, here I was hanging to hear your voice and that's the first thing you say? Well I'm doing shit here thanks for asking. Days are long. Food is shit. I'm sharing a room with a heavy snorer and it's hot as fuck. Thanks. How's the mansion you're in?'

Survival #3: Lean on your friends. Have a core group you can rely on.

I didn't sleep all night. When his swing finished, I was waiting at the arrival hall at the airport and when he hugged me, my stress melted away. I felt safe again. That night in the bedroom, he tried a new move. I was pretty horny so I went with it and let him lead. And then the next swing, he tried a different move; in fact, four new ones that swing. It wasn't until the next swing when he tried to lightly choke me I realised that something was up. He stopped mid-bang as I froze and he asked if I was okay. I asked what was going on. As I said before, missionary was pretty much my only move. Pete is the only guy I've been with and vice versa. I asked him what was up with the new moves. He simply replied with something like, 'I've got so much spare time to think, I thought I'd plan some new moves for the bedroom!' It played on my mind all week. One day when I was supposed to be at work, I came home early to surprise him with Buffalo wings and beer. It was me that got the surprise though. I walked in to hear loud moaning and groaning. Pleasure yells, squealing 'Yes baby deeper, deeper.' My heart froze. This couldn't be happening. My picture perfect life was crumbling right in front of me. I hastily followed the moans to the theatre room. And there he was ... butt naked, on the couch with his throbbing boner gripped tightly in his hand. He was watching porn on the big screen. Besides being a bit offended that perhaps my efforts weren't good enough for him, I laughed it off and joined in on the fun.

> **Misconception #1: 'You can afford that, your husband works away' – that doesn't mean money grows on trees FML.**

'It's what guys do Stacey,' I assured myself. But it was the extent he was doing it - I didn't think that would be classed as normal. Over the next five months I would catch him wanking in multiple places; even in my parents' house on the toilet. That was the final straw for me. It was time to confront him. He denied that he had an addiction and all the boys did it on-site. I asked him how often he did it on-site, and he brushed it off saying 'not much, just like one or two times a week if I'm having trouble sleeping.' Little old innocent me believed him and I brushed it off too. Swing after swing, the crazy new sex moves would be introduced into our bedroom. It was beginning to feel like high school sex, all about the man and awkward AF. I mean why would I want to wrap my legs behind my head whilst he jumps on the bed, in me. He could feel my stiffness and that I wasn't into the weird shit, so he pulled back. The next swing, we didn't even have sex. I felt shit. Unwanted. Unsexy. I asked him if he was seeing someone else. He denied it and said he just wasn't feeling horny, he was 'too tired.' Catering to my man, I again believed him. After a few months, it started getting to me. We hadn't had sex in almost nine months. There had to be something going on.

On the next fly-in day, I decided to initiate sexy time. I went to Bras N Things and got something a little sexier than my '5 for $30' Cotton On undies. He was reluctant to entertain me, so I just grabbed him and threw him down on the couch. I started to perform oral, (I can count on my hands how many times I'd done it before that time). He seemed to really enjoy it and grabbed the back of my head and started thrusting. I choked. I pulled back and said, 'What the hell are you doing?!'

Misconception #2: 'Hubby is on holiday when he is back.' Not true, I put his ass to work!

He stormed off into the bathroom ... with his phone. I laid in bed crying as he was wanking in our guest bathroom. I fell asleep and woke in the middle of the night. He wasn't in bed. I went to look for him and found him in the office with headphones on, chatting on webcam to a working girl. I could not believe my eyes. I grabbed the laptop and threw it on the floor. I was raging. My self-esteem was at an all-time low and this guy was sitting in our house wanking over some slut on the computer. He refused to talk. He brushed it all off saying I was overexaggerating. He assured me that was his first time on the webcam. He only looks at porn every other day. I was sobbing. Uncontrollably. He grabbed and held me in his arms and carried me to bed. He was flying out that morning so I didn't want to waste any time fighting. We made love. Sweet love. Soft, gentle, missionary love. He promised he wasn't going to look at porn anymore. I believed him. Of course I did. My high school sweetheart would never break a promise.

This swing was a little different. I willingly became the porn star. I surprised him with a nude selfie. I initiated some phone sex. I giggled through most of it, but hey, I tried. I was confident he wouldn't need to watch random Big Booty girls on his phone anymore. Feeling terrible (and super sexy at this point), I got his laptop fixed before he got home. I was going to make my own home movie with him. Again, innocent me went to his search bar to find a 'program for video editing' and before I could even type in the R in program, an overwhelming history for porn sites appeared. And that was it. I fell into a rabbit hole of delving into his search history. His google account is linked to his phone and I saw that he looked at porn ('Anna gets banged by her neighbour' to be exact), as soon as he got off the phone to me. He told me that he had finished, why would he need to be aroused again? Did he lie? Was he finished with my immature attempt at phone sex? I texted him and asked him if he looked at porn today. He flat out lied and said, 'Babe, your pics are more than enough.' Would you believe after that call, he went and watched another one? He searched porn movies a minimum of nine times a day. EVERYDAY.

> Misconception #3: 'I don't know how you can be away from each other for so long.' Sure we miss each other however this is a short term sacrifice we both agreed on.

Let's just say naïve Stacey was gone and this swing, I was swinging shots at his manhood. I had all the evidence I needed and he couldn't tell me otherwise. He was a porn addict. He had a sex addiction. He was unsatisfied with me, the good wife, because his fantasy of a porn star experience was not being met. His unrealistic expectations were created on-site, from all the porn he was watching. I told him I was going to leave him if he didn't get help. He reluctantly agreed. Apparently this is a super common issue couples face with the FIFO lifestyle. The instant gratification of clicking a link and getting your rocks off was ruining the intimacy at home. No foreplay needed because porn stars were always ready for a good time.

After a few setbacks, falling into old routines and loneliness, we are finally in a good place. Sexually and mentally. His sex therapist has set some steps for him to follow should he feel vulnerable. She also gave us tips as a couple to keep sexual cravings satisfied. Strangely enough, she suggested we watch porn together, but specific realistic ones. Not Jenna Jamison ones. I have to admit, it's pretty fun and we have explored a whole new realm of sexual activity. We even have a little collection of toys, pleasurable for the both of us. He's been clean for eighteen months now and I hope I'm not being naïve again, but I believe this time is different. I sure bloody hope so!

My advice for couples struggling with bedroom drama is to keep it sexy. Just keep it fun and never say no. Once you start saying 'no', is when they start to look at ways to fill their void. Send nudes. Send videos. Make good use of FaceTime. Go on dates. Have dress ups. Get some toys. Be open with your desires and don't be afraid to go for it.

'IT'S NOT THE LIFE I WOULD HAVE CHOSEN, BUT IT'S HIS CAREER CHOICE SO I SUPPORT HIM, BECAUSE HE WOULD DO THE SAME FOR ME. I STILL HAVE FEELINGS OF RESENTMENT SOMETIMES, BUT I MANAGE THEM AS THEY ARISE. IT'S MOSTLY AROUND SOLO PARENTING. THERE'S NO ONE THERE AT THE END OF THE DAY TO TAKE THE REIGNS, AND I'M ALWAYS 'PUSHING THROUGH' AND FEELING BURNT OUT. SELF CARE IS INCREDIBLY IMPORTANT TO MY SANITY.'

Sarah Dlugosz – 'The Understanding Wife'

THE UNDERSTANDING WIFE

Name: Sarah Dlugosz
Industry: Underground Mining
Relationship Status: Married 9 Years
Time in Industry: 10 years

M ining has been a part of my family for a long time. Mum's family grew up in Kalgoorlie and my uncles worked in mining for as long as I've known them. My sister works in mining admin and I started working FIFO in 2006. It all started for me when my best friend showed up on my doorstep and told me she had found some cheap flights to Europe and we were leaving in five months. Another friend of mine, who was also coming to Europe with us, was already working on the mines making good coin, so I knew it was the best way to make some fast cash. Over the next five months, I managed to save $13,000, 7000 of which I earnt in my final five-week swing. That was big coin for a twenty-three-year-old female with no formal education, however, it was incredibly isolating and there were many nights I cried myself to sleep.

Being a woman on the mines, it was smart to avoid communal spaces as much as possible. I remember walking into a huge bar of a 2500-man camp and instantly drawing looks, wolf whistles and a lot of unwanted attention. I turned around and went straight back to my room. My friend had a man walk up to her in the mess, sniff her, and say 'Woman,' like a proper caveman. Luckily we ended up on our last swing together and that helped us get through it. Having a goal made it so much easier. My best friend decorated my room with pictures of Europe one day while I was on shift; it was such a nice surprise, and really helped me focus on our end goal.

> Survival #1: When he first comes home, tell him exactly where the kids are at. Kids can change a lot in a week. He would sometimes come home trying to do things that worked last time that I KNEW wouldn't work anymore. So a family update, and tips on how to deal with certain behaviours the kids will throw at him are a must to help him brace for what's to come.

At the end of our last swing, we tied the shoe laces of our boots together and tossed them up in a tree, and then ripped our uniform to shreds. We couldn't be happier to never be going back. So in May 2007 we left for Europe with no real plans and no idea how long we'd be away.

Within the first two weeks of what ended up being a nineteen-month trip, I met my husband Micolaj on the dance floor of a dungeon drum and bass club in Krakow. Little did we know it was the start of a lot of 'long distance' love and the rest of our lives together. I spent the next year travelling and maintaining a relationship with him. We only saw each other once a month until he moved to London to live with me in May 2008. Five months later my working visa expired and I was running out of money, so I had to head home. I was ecstatic when he proposed to me shortly before I left London and said he wanted to come to Australia with me. I arrived back in Perth in November 2008 wondering what the fuck I was doing! If I wasn't engaged, I'd be heading straight back to the mines to make more coin and hit the road again, but when he arrived in Perth in January 2009, we were so excited to start our lives in Australia together.

Micolaj had worked on machinery in Poland, making the equivalent of AU$500 a month, so when I told him about the money he could be make on the mines, he was keen! Once he had working rights and his HR license, he easily got a job thanks to my connections. He thought he was a millionaire when he started bringing in $500 a day! I remember asking him each payday what he made, and every time, he would raise his pinky finger to his lips like Dr. Evil, and tell me, 'ONE MILLION DOLLARS.' He literally felt like a millionaire. Problem was, he started spending it like he was rich (and he actually wasn't) haha. He had never had much money growing up, so he had to learn how to manage it. Lucky I'm Dutch and an avid saver, so I could teach him about budgeting, but he also taught me to be more generous and spontaneous.

> **Survival #2: Don't be afraid to go to counselling! We have a wonderful relationship therapist that we turn to when things get rocky between us. She has brought us back from the brink of divorce a few times. We are back seeing her now as we find we use all our energy for the kids during the day and when they go to bed, we both just want to do our own thing. Maybe it's what we're used to due to our time apart, but it's not good for reconnecting on his weeks at home.**

I had financially supported us since we first met, and Micolaj was very happy to finally be the provider. His wages allowed for me to go to university for four years to complete my BA Psychology and Counselling, while only working a few casual hours a week. Studying while he was away was a great distraction as I needed a lot of alone time to read text books and write assignments, and it proved beneficial as I graduated with first class honours in 2012.

Our financial freedom also allowed us to travel to Europe

a number of times to see his family and explore new countries together. When we finally wed in February 2012, we were able to support ten of his friends and family to fly to Perth for the wedding. We were then able to save enough for a house deposit in the next ten months, and bought our first home together by the end of 2012, on one main wage. On the outside, it looked like we had the perfect relationship, but there were a number of challenges due to the FIFO lifestyle.

> **Survival #3:** Be respectful of each others roles. It's not a competition of who's got it hardest. You're a team, so act like it! Have each other's backs; share the load when he's home. And for any FIFO hubbies reading this ... give her a day to herself without her having to ask! Book her a massage! Send her flowers on special occasions! Let her know you love and appreciate her, and she will be aching to see you, and do all the naughty things to you when you walk through that door :)

When I remember back to those first few years of 2:1 FIFO life, I think of the challenges our relationship went through. His first stint was remote, with no phone or internet connection. We could only talk via the company's satellite phone, which was expensive, so calls had to be kept to a minimum. We would speak only a few minutes every few days. Communication was minimal which felt out of our control. When he did finally make it to a mine site, he was happy to keep to minimal contact, which baffled me. I remember saying, 'This is not okay!' and him genuinely not realising that. We had to have many discussions about our expectations of the FIFO lifestyle and our relationship within it.

I remember him flying in from his swing and telling me he had made plans to go out that night, drinking with a mate. I felt hurt he didn't want to hang with me as much as I was wanting to be with him. When he came home drunk, I told him that it wasn't acceptable, and that we needed time to reconnect first. Thankfully he agreed with me when I spelled things out to him, but there were many times I've had to do that.

With such limited time together, we would spend most of his break doing things as a couple, with and without friends. We spent all our time together, which maybe isn't realistic for a relationship, but we'd already spent so much time apart. I can see now that I had co-dependence in the early years; I missed my best friend and lover like crazy, feeling like a piece of me was gone when he was away. I was pining and longing for him. I am reminded of these feelings from old Facebook memories, like this one:

I exhale the words,
'I want my husband'
Subconsciously, repeatedly.
Not letting me forget;
My heart is crying,
My body's denied,
Without your hands on me.
(2013)

I remember crying as I drove him to the airport thinking that I wasn't good enough for him to want to find work in Perth and come home to me each night. I can see now this was my own abandonment wound, due to having an absent father, playing out in my relationship. I see now this experience was a blessing in disguise as it gave me the opportunity to heal these wounds and I'm happy to say, they are no longer an issue for me.

We started trying to conceive our first child in 2013, which proved more difficult than we realised. Trying to line up my fertile window with a 2:1 roster meant many missed opportunities. It dragged out to three years of trying for a baby and had a huge impact on our relationship. We had given up partying, and took up beach running, playing tennis, hiking and other active sports; we were having fun and feeling healthy and fit. But then Micolaj tore his ACL while Judo training. Due to needing six weeks off work for the surgery, it just hasn't happened yet, but it meant we could no longer keep up our healthy activities.

> **Misconception #1:** When hubby was looking for jobs, 2:1 rosters were advertised as 'family friendly rosters.' No family should have to be apart more than they are together, that is NOT family friendly.

We became increasingly depressed and sex became a chore, with us both starting to question if we were happy in the relationship. We had drifted apart. I was resenting Micolaj working away, wishing he would come home, but this was his career choice and he wasn't going to change it anytime soon. We had a discussion over the phone about breaking up and decided to give it six more months. I remember saying 'If we're meant to stay together, we'll fall pregnant,' and Micolaj was angry, saying our relationship needed work before we brought a child into it. Well, two weeks later while Micolaj was away at work, I took a pregnancy test, expecting a negative result, as I had seen too many times. When it was positive, it was a strange feeling, because Micolaj and I weren't in a good place. I texted him and told him to call me as soon as he woke up, so I could tell him the good news. He was shocked but happy; it felt so strange to not be physically together when we finally got the news we'd been waiting for. A beautiful moment for connection, missed ...

I was brought up by my single mother and had told Micolaj I didn't want to be a FIFO parent, essentially a single parent half my life. He agreed and when Lena was born in January 2017, he started a job in Perth. I admired Micolaj's enthusiasm and attempt at a new job, but door-to-door sales of solar was never going to work for him. The highs and lows of good weeks and bad weeks meant income was inconsistent and he felt he couldn't provide for his family. I was on maternity leave and we had to defer our mortgage at one point, as things got that tight. He then got a job working long hours in a cardboard factory, which paid well but took its toll with the early mornings and sixty-hour weeks. I could see this job was sucking the life and joy out of him. He wasn't happy, and when he suffers, so does our relationship.

> **Misconception #2: That FIFO families are rich! Umm, no. Far from it. We can put a little extra away each pay to go towards weekends away etc, but we still have bills to pay and live in a small 3x1 house. Yes, our only debt is the mortgage, but that's because we're smart with our money.**

I distinctly remember the moment he told me he was going back to FIFO, because I had such a strong reaction to it. I literally fell to the floor in tears. All I could think about was not coping as a solo parent, and falling into dark depression. He thought I was over-reacting, but it was a very real fear for me. He was adamant that this was what he wanted, but the only way I could agree to it was by making him promise that if I wasn't coping he would try working in Perth again. I remember feeling it was his happiness over mine. I felt coerced into a life I didn't want, but if it meant having a happy husband, it was a sacrifice I was willing to make. I had one stipulation though: it had to be even time.

Despite years in the industry and making it to senior roles, there were no even time rosters for his skill set. So, to get even time, he had to start his career over, at the bottom. This meant a pay cut, even from the factory job, and a 2:2 roster. Thankfully I was back at work so we could make ends meet, but it didn't feel worth it to me. Then I fell pregnant again (thankfully quite easily thanks to a better roster), and we both knew something had to change. He had been applying for 1:1 jobs and while he was home awaiting the arrival of our second daughter, he got a call offering him the role he'd been manifesting; more money and week on, week off. I was so proud of him for sticking to his guns and getting what he wanted. I could live with this.

However, I remember the first year of my second daughter, Amelia's, life for all the wrong reasons. I was worn out from doing sleepless nights solo, then solo parenting through the day. I became the parent I never wanted to be, and saw the impact of this on my eldest daughter, whose behaviour became more and more challenging. Though any more than a week with Micolaj away would have been really hard, one week of him home wasn't enough.

He would fly-in on a Tuesday, so Wednesdays were always a write-off. My eldest daughter would meltdown all day, not coping with the change of daddy being home. She would resist him and not want him to help her, but deep down I could see she was hurt because he had been away. By the end of his week home, we would have recalibrated and be enjoying life as a family, then BAM! He was gone again. I really struggled to create any kind of rythym in our household for a long time. However, with a four-year-old and twenty-one-month-old, I feel like I'm starting to get it. However, Micolaj still struggled with home life sometimes.

I remember Micolaj bringing home some HARD energies, like I could tell he'd been at the pub with his mates most nights during his swing. He was defensive, would swear a lot and not be nice to be around, not like the guy I married. He was short with the kids; they would get upset and I'd have to put out the fires. There were many times I resented him because not only did I have to contain the kids' behaviour, I had to contain his too. There were weeks I didn't miss him, because when he was home, life was harder, like I had another child to look after. We had a big chat and I helped him realise he had been embracing the 'single' lifestyle with no responsibilities once he knocked off, and hanging with his mates. When he came home, he would feel like he couldn't 'knock off' or relax and resented the hard work of raising kids. No wonder we didn't want him around, it was because he didn't want to be around us. We finally agreed that when he went to work, that was his 'break', and when he came home he was 'on' because we both agreed that consciously raising two little ones was the FUCKING HARDEST THING WE'VE EVER DONE! Once he was able to switch this around in his head, and become aware of how he was unconsciously responding to the challenges of fatherhood, he was able to be a better dad, and more supportive husband.

> **Misconception #3:** 'You don't lose your wife, you just lose your turn.' This is what one of my FIFO ex-boyfriends told me once. I was horrified that men spoke like that on the mines. There is definitely more opportunities to cheat when you're away from each other, but if you're doing enough to keep your relationship healthy, then trust issues don't need to be a problem. My hubby and I have an agreement to talk to each other if we're having thoughts about being with someone else. We agree its normal and healthy to look, but not to act.

One thing I still don't think he understands is just how much his job choice affects my life. I too, have to live a FIFO life. Before I can respond to any invites to events, or plan my own, I am forever checking his roster. The joy I feel when he is home when I need him, is awesome, but the disappointment I feel when I have to say 'Hubby's not home, I can't come' SUCKS! I don't have a lot of people I can call on to babysit, and I don't want to push my luck with the ones I can call. And no one likes going to weddings or parties alone ... so there's a lot I miss out on. I know Micolaj misses things too, and that's just part of this lifestyle, however this isn't MY choice. It is his.

I would love to have a daily morning ritual of meditation and yoga, but as a solo mum, this is unattainable. I'm too tired after night wakes to wake up before them (would have to be 4 am!), and I have demands thrown at me before I've even opened my eyes. I have seen how much this would improve my life, as I was able to do it during COVID with him home, and it was transformational. When he is home I try to do it, but it's in stolen moments. I really wish he would say 'Babe, I've got the kids for the next hour, go do what you need,' but I'm yet to hear this, and I'm not very good at asking for it either.

Then there's the reality that I know the kids better; they prefer me when they're upset, or to read their bedtime book, and sing them their favourite song. I know other families that take turns with bedtimes etc., but that's not possible for us, as the kids always want mama. Micolaj is a great dad, but can miss their cues, misunderstand their needs, and have less patience with them, because his parenting is interrupted by work, they feel that and prefer me. I KNOW this wouldn't be the case if he worked in Perth, because when he has them for the two days I work, I see them shift towards him more. But then he flies back and the pattern begins all over again.

My friends call me a superwoman because they don't know how I do what I do. When I have long sleepless nights juggling one child spewing while changing the other kid's bedsheets at midnight, or early wakes with one child after the other has kept me awake half the night, it's hard not to resent him for choosing this job. Having to do two drop-offs and pick-ups on the days I work, then coming home and cooking dinner and doing bath and bedtime solo, collapsing on the couch, hoping I get some decent rest before doing it again the next day. You have to be really organised for FIFO life with kids, and I am not that person. I know as the kids get older, it will get easier and I will have more freedom, but while I'm in it, it feels like my life isn't my own, that I am living to keep everyone else happy.

But the perks aren't lost on me. Micolaj has since moved to another mine site, with a promotion and more money, and a goal firmly in sight to go higher. We don't have our dream home yet, but we can afford to take family trips in our old caravan on his weeks off, and spend silly amounts of money on alternative practitioners and remedies – homeopathy, kinesiology, bodytalk, massage – all of which are essential for my self-care to help me cope with this lifestyle.

I seem to have figured out how to make a FIFO family work, for now, despite the challenges. We still have our moments, and are actually in a bit of a funk right now, but we will get through it, as we always do. As long as he is happy, and treating us well, then I can do this as long as he needs.

'IT TAKES COURAGE TO LIVE BOLDLY. THIS
LIFESTYLE MAKES YOU LOVE, FORGIVE, AND TRY
AGAIN; YOU FEEL FEAR, BUT YOU DO IT ANYWAY.
YOU FIND OUT THAT SOMETIMES THE SMALLEST
STEP IN THE RIGHT DIRECTION ENDS UP BEING THE
BIGGEST ONE. YOU DARE TO APPEAR ON THE STAGE
OF LIFE AND MAKE SURE YOUR SOUL IS HAPPY.
EASY? NOT AT ALL, BUT REMEMBER, LIFE DOES NOT
DEMAND PERFECTION.'

Pryscyla Campbell – 'The Stormy Wife'

THE STORMY WIFE

NAME: PRYSCYLA CAMPBELL
INDUSTRY: IRON ORE
RELATIONSHIP STATUS: MARRIED
TIME IN INDUSTRY: 13 YEARS

I arrived in Australia in 2006 from Brazil. I came later in life; I was thirty-five years old when I decided to have a new adventure. As any migrant knows, it's hard to start over. I was prepared to enjoy as many new experiences as I could. I did all types of work to be able to support myself and pay for university. As an international student, the cost of education can be up to three times more than local students. I did not have any spare time to date. When things started to calm down, I thought, okay, let's see what we have out there. I travelled to a few places by myself or with a group of friends; I really enjoyed knowing I could do that.

When my husband and I first started to date I had no idea what a FIFO life meant, although it did not seem to affect my routine. Honestly, I really enjoyed it. I still had time to myself, to go out with friends, and I was working full-time and in the last year of university. With my (then) boyfriend gone for a week or two, I was able to dedicate myself to my work, uni and social life. We met later in life. With a mature mind and a clear vision about what we wanted in a relationship, we had an open conversation about the pros and cons of FIFO life and just a few months later, we decided to live together. As I said before, little changed. We enjoyed each other's company and I always believe that when you are a couple, conversation and companionship are essential. We travel a lot and enjoy every minute. He got a fright though when we travelled to Brazil for my sister's wedding, and finally met my family. I had told him that I have a big family, but when we arrived there, he saw more than a hundred people wanting to meet him - he froze! But he soon got over that.

> **Survival #1: Have a plan, plan your week, make sure you have time to look after yourself.**

When he proposed, it was beautiful. We decided to get married in New Zealand and organise the wedding within three months, after we had a holiday stop-over there. We visited some places and chose the date after our second visit, and then informed our families. A few of the family members from Brazil came to our wedding. It was a beachfront wedding on a beautiful day. Funny, as I am writing this, my wedding anniversary is in just a few days.

Because of our age, we decided not to wait too long to have a baby. Unfortunately, it wasn't long before we had our first miscarriage, which was not a good moment for us. We phoned each other many times a day and supported each other as much as possible with him working away. I did not have any family here and the grieving process was challenging. Yes, I do have good friends, so don't get me wrong, I did really appreciate their support, but it's not the same as family. Miscarriage is not something that people talk openly about; it is still a taboo subject. We then started our IVF journey. Consultations, hormones, right days to try, more hormones, cycle failures. Big note here, we women feel really crap with all these hormones in our body and mind, and sometimes we can really lose it - when it happens, it's not a beautiful picture. I am so grateful that my husband was able to deal with me. I became a 'wifezilla' under those circumstances. As time marched on with ups and downs on the treatment, we decided to have a second honeymoon. I went to the doctor and said, 'I need you to stimulate my ovaries, nature will take care of the rest.' I was over the continuous roller coaster of emotions. We enjoyed the trip a lot; relaxing times, new places, new experiences. Back home and back to FIFO life, I was working full-time, and had my final month of university; the routine was back.

Four weeks later, we got news of a baby on the way. I had a great pregnancy if you consider that the doctor considered me 'old' to have a baby. I was forty years old when my daughter was born. During the pregnancy I worked until the end of thirty-eight weeks, and I finished my degree before the birth. Then the significant changes started.

Survival #2: Never put yourself in second place ... like the instruction on the plane, put the oxygen mask on you first.

I chose to be a stay-at-home mum. We, as a couple, decided it would be fine if I took time off to be a mum. In the beginning, it was great; I loved being with my baby and I joined a great mother's group. What I ignored was that I was with these mums just once a week, and after that, I was on my own. I did have friends, but they were in a different moment in life. I did not count on the loneliness, or the stress and how much these affected my life and my relationship with myself and my husband. Man, he is not perfect, but he was there to back me up when I needed help. Ten months after my daughter was born, I was pregnant again. Another miscarriage emotionally put me down. The fact my husband was away contributed to the toll and the fear; self-doubt and lack of self-esteem increased. I am a mum, and my baby still needed care, so I just kept going. This period was not an easy one. After that we did more rounds of IVF; this was like a bomb of hormones on my body and I was on a roller coaster of emotions - to put it mildly, it was hell. At this time, our lives were run by the what ifs; What if I am pregnant, I cannot do this? What if I have another miscarriage? What if I can't cope with more kids? What if this and what if that.

> **Survival #3: Do not be too hard on yourself; it's okay not to be okay sometimes.**

Our family life basically disappeared in the midst of it all. We had five more miscarriages. My husband was sometimes home, sometimes away, and we would cry over the phone throughout the process. He, too, was suffering and it hit him hard. The grieving did not become easier, but you develop coping mechanisms that may mask or hide the issues. I think that was one of the signals that I missed in looking for help earlier.

One day, I was by myself, and I had one of those 'moments.' What the hell are you doing with your life? You have a great husband and a daughter you love, and they love you; why are you not enjoying it? It was hard to look in the mirror and recognise that I was not giving value to what I already had, and seeing that my wanting was playing a part in it. At that moment I realised I had to decide if I would continue to live on the what ifs. Having an eternal doubt about being a mother again, I was sure I was not being the best I could be for my daughter and husband. I was not living in the moment. Accepting that I may not have another child was hard because that moment made me feel like a failure as a woman. How could I be a good mother, a good wife? I needed to change my whole belief system.

When my husband came home that swing it was time for the hard conversation. We dropped off our daughter to the day care and went for a coffee. In that conversation, I told him all my thoughts, feelings, anxieties; I just put all the crap out there. I asked him how he was feeling and his opinion. Open heart conversations like these shake a lot inside and hit hard on some of your intrinsic beliefs. It was the hardest conversation I ever had in my life, and I imagine it was for him as well. By the end of it, we decided to hear an opinion from a different doctor and we would make a decision after that.

Visiting the doctor and telling him our history and explaining why we were there was hard. The first question the doctor asked, 'Mum, are you sleeping well?' I laugh inside, as I am a mother, and you and I know what that means. I was firm that I would open up and be honest, and I told the truth ... a big fat NO. He said, 'First things first, we are going to help you fix that, and in the meantime, we do the tests.' I suddenly felt okay for the first time in three years. It was like he took a big load off. During the month waiting for the results, we did something that we had not done for years, we took time off as a family, and really enjoyed it. For me, it was an eye-opener to realise that, yes, I do have a great family. Then the results came back that I did not have any egg reserve. With that, we decided not to have another child and just enjoy the beauty of life, just the three of us.

Misconception #1: 'Money pays for all the difficult times.'

That result helped me to appreciate the family I have. We now make our holidays a great event with all three of us involved in planning it, and I value more and more the time we spend together. We celebrate the little and the big victories that each of us has. Seeing the bright smile on my daughter's face, my husband's smile, and my eyes full of life again is priceless.

When you became a mother, you add more and more hats.

What I mean is we have to be so many people; mother, wife, woman. We end up not valuing some of those areas. I was lost; I lost my identity as a woman, an independent human being able to make decisions on my own. It's hard to admit it, but these admissions were the starting point for me to reinvent myself. Some people might say that it was too late for me to do that, keeping in mind I was in my early forties. And for a while, the movie of my life played in my head over and over to add to the fear, self-doubt, and lack of courage; low self-esteem became a permanent companion. There is a voice in all of us that at certain times will say:

- Who do you think you are to do new things?

- What are people going to say?

- You will fail if you try it …

And the doubting voice goes on and on and on … no one ever suspected because I always had a big smile on my face. I call it the 'enough moment.' This moment happened when the results of my egg reserve came back. We made some decisions that changed our lives.

Misconception #2: 'You can't complain, your life is the dream.'

Our daughter was born during our FIFO life. When she was smaller, we didn't have any problems. We used to put one of dad's t-shirts over a pillow inside her cot, so she always had dad's smell close to her. I imagine it was not easy for dad to be away from his baby girl, but as she grew, she started to miss her father more. Once, he worked away for eight weeks. At the end of this period, she began developing a 'psychological fever.' I took her to the doctor almost every day for a week because her fever did not go down. We did every test, and all came back normal, but less than twelve hours after her dad got home all the symptoms were gone, not a single sign of the drama I had endured by myself. Side note: I needed a lot of patience with myself and her, and I still do not think that it was fair on me - mummy's thoughts!

Misconception #3: 'It's so easy for you, you get to stay home.'

As a family, we have always had an open dialogue about how we feel. Of course that sometimes means we have an argument or two, after all, we are two different people from two different families with different cultures. When you put all these differences together in a bag and shake really well, you have us, and that is how we operate. My husband and I are very serious about respect. We are not allowed to disrespect each other, and we explain that to our daughter, who is now eight years old. This is one of the values that we want her to have for life; you are not obligated to agree with other people's opinions, but you need to respect their choices. I asked her how she feels about her dad working way because her well-being matters. She says that sometimes it is hard because she misses his cuddles, but then she said if he was here all the time, we couldn't have our girls' nights. The girls in this house go out when in the mood, and we prepare fine dining at home too. These are some examples of rituals that I create with my daughter to show her that it is okay to do things with one parent. She and her dad also have their own things where mum is not allowed.

Some people say that you have to find balance in your life, and I believe you have to give the appropriate attention to the part of your life that is in need. That does not mean that you will let the rest run loose, it means that you will focus on what's important and it will positively impact others. When I look after myself, my family is happier, and my other hats are running fine; I am a better woman, a better wife and a much better mum.

FIFO life is a choice that we make as a family. It has pros and cons, and they vary according to the moment in your life. It has its good, and it has its not so good moments. Unfortunately, from the outside, a lot of people have a misconception that the good money pays for all we have to endure and sacrifice as a family.

Easy? Of course not; it is a daily choice that I make for my well-being. Some days are harder than others. I choose to keep moving forward.

'IT TAKES TWO OF YOU TO KEEP MOVING FORWARD; TO SUPPORT, TO BE HONOURABLE, TO BE THE STRENGTH FOR THE OTHER WHEN NEEDED. WE WEREN'T BORN ASSUMING TO BE PERFECT, BUT WE CAN STRIVE FOR PROGRESSION OF PERFECTION WITH THE RIGHT HUMAN BY OUR SIDE.'

Melissa Hamer – 'The I Swiped Right Wife'

THE I SWIPED RIGHT WIFE

Name: Melissa Hamer
Industry: Mining
Relationship Status: Married (newly ... 2 months)
Time in Industry: 9 years

It was 2013.

He shouldn't have stood out in my memory, as it was a music festival filled with similar people wondering the grounds, yet ... he did.

A mohawk, a suit vest (with no shirt underneath) and a tie.

I was in a crochet tank top, a floppy (dorky – his words) hat and hair that is completely opposite to who I am today.

I was waiting by myself for Motion City Soundtrack to come out for their set, while his band was finishing up ... but we wouldn't say hello and introduce ourselves for another three years in 2016, and it wouldn't be until 2019 at my sister's baby shower, that he would remind me of this shared moment I had pushed to the back of my mind.

2016 - My heart had just been broken. I was dealing with selling a house and everything else that comes with that era ending. My confidence was completely shot and I didn't see myself wanting to be in a relationship ever again.

My best friend told me I just needed to put myself back out there and join Tinder. I was very apprehensive about it as that was pretty much the nail in the coffin with my previous relationship.

Her words repeated in my head over and over as I downloaded the app, setting up my profile, wondering if this really was the best thing to do.

> **Survival #1: Talk everyday. Although it's not every hour, we aim to have a phone call every night (sure there are times that this doesn't happen ... because well ... life & different time zones, exhaustion), but hearing their voice on the other end of the phone each night makes a world of difference for each of you.**

I had figured out a little cheat or algorithm with Tinder, that if you had been swiped right on, they would keep coming up in your searches until you swiped left or right.

After reading this guy's profile ... this tattooed, scotch and coffee drinking, rockabilly music loving guy grabbed my attention, but then I saw his last photo ... and couldn't decide on left or right, so I closed my phone.

Our profiles should have never passed one another, we should have never met – but I do believe in fate.

We lived on opposite sides of the city, out of the love searching 150km radius radar.

I would have been working in the studio in Melbourne while Luke was waiting at Melbourne Airport for his flight out to site.

After a week of deciding on which way to swipe on the 'Star Wars guy,' right I swiped.

Surprise, surprise, we matched.

After a week of texting, we decided to catch up for a coffee. After running forty-five minutes late (oops! just setting the expectations of a life with me from the beginning), coffee turned into dinner and a few scotches and wines (and no coffees) and four hours of non-stop conversation.

Luke started telling me about his job as a FIFO worker, and all I could do was think back to my hospitality days of 'First In First Out.'

Luke had told me that he had been single for a few years (lucky for me), as he explained that not many girls were interested in dating a guy that was never around.

So for the next four years, I learnt what the FIFO life was all about; all of the testing and emotional ups and downs, the many alone times, birthdays and Christmases apart, the countless nights going to bed on the phone, waking up in the morning to an empty bed but a good morning message, forever explaining to everyone where he was, why he works away, why I am with him, no I don't want someone else, and that I don't have to justify my relationship.

I found myself constantly advising people that while mining is good money, Luke wasn't bringing in a million a swing, like everyone assumed!

I would never say that being with a FIFO worker is a walk in the park, but after my previous relationship, and having the feeling of wasting seven years of my life with the wrong person, I would rather be apart from the right guy, then spend all my time with the wrong one.

> Survival #2: Try and stick to your usual routine while your human is home; it makes it easier to fall back into some sort of normality when they fly back to site.

It's that feeling of almost five years together, (now driving to the airport to collect him), still having butterflies in your stomach and feel the smile coming from your eyes, knowing that you are about to see him for the first time in two weeks.

You become their personal life assistant in a way. I absolutely support him in his career, and to better himself and for us, but to say it has been easy would be straight-out lying through my teeth.

It's spending three hours a day in peak-hour traffic, working a full time job, being overwhelmed by life, putting on a brave face at a family gathering without them, coming home to an empty house AGAIN, finding the strength to cook dinner for one, laying in bed and forgetting that you haven't put the bins out (even after being reminded), wanting to cry into your pillow because of the day you've had, and just be held as you fall asleep. But waking up the following morning and telling yourself he is freaking worth it and doing it worse than you!

You have to fight battles alone, where you really wish they were there physically to do it with you.

Living the FIFO life isn't something most people would voluntarily sign up for at the start of a relationship. For the majority of the time, it's a joint couple/family decision, made after discussing goals, the future, houses and holidays.

I unknowingly signed up to that lifestyle the night I swiped right!

Luke working 2:1 swings from Melbourne meant it was more of an extension of the two weeks away and less than the one week home, due to travel time. The time difference between Victoria and Western Australia was also a big factor in our relationship, especially when daylight savings came in.

Breakfast was lunch, dinner was bed time, I've always joked that 'hello, goodbye' by the Beatles was the FIFO life song.

This all changed dramatically, as for the next four years, Luke began completing a TAFE up-skill course through work, to open up further opportunities and to be able to provide for us more as a family moving forward.

All of his TAFE modules were on his week off, when he was meant to be back in Victoria.

His 2:1's quickly and regularly turned into 5:1's and 8:1's and even one 12:1. You feel alone, and yet feel like a sook if you complain about your loneliness. You start to justify your feelings as unwarranted, especially as they are doing it worse.

I became both envious and infuriated by the girls I worked with, who complained when they didn't hear back from a text from their partner for thirty minutes, whereas, I would send a message at 5 am, and hear nothing for twelve or thirteen hours, but as the saying goes, 'You just do you.'

There have been multiple times when Luke has been so exhausted he would message me after work with my usual, 'Hello baby,' then he would have dinner in his room and fall asleep before he could even get to call me. Yes, it does hurt and is a short shot of disappointment, but it's just what it is.

Sometimes you get to the point of missing someone so much, that you legitimately cannot speak once the nightly conversation starts - you are both exhausted and know it. So you just sit there with one another on the phone in silence, watching TV like you would in the same room on the couch in a 'normal relationship' – whatever that is?

I'm sure you've heard the rumour, that's often been drilled into me; 'FIFO's always cheat.' But I have never had any of those thoughts cross my mind. The level of trust, loyalty and respect Luke and I have always had for one another has been something I cherish.

Perspective, dream vacays, future goals, the 'dream home' is what kept us going every swing, and every moment we spent apart. Then after Luke proposed on our block of land in 2018, the dream wedding in Uluwatu, Bali in 2020 and the build of our home, was what kept us working hard together and (mostly) apart.

Then, COVID hit!

... We lost our wedding six weeks out, as soon as international borders were closed and travel was stopped. Then Victoria went into lockdown on my birthday (dad gave me toilet paper as a present), all while Luke was stuck on-site on the other side of the country.

My soul was absolutely crushed. I didn't think it could get much worse but then they started closing businesses and I lost both of my jobs as a personal trainer and group instructor.

After spending three-and-a-half hours on the phone to an airline to try and change a flight to come home, throwing down a small fortune, Luke made it home to his broken fiancé.

The trip home would only be for a mini-second, and the start of a new set of challenges for the both of us.

Forced with the tough decision to keep our duo family going through this new unknown pandemic, we both knew that Luke had to go back to Western Australia, we just weren't expecting it to be the next day (and not being able to complete the new Netflix series 'Tiger King'). We were told it was 'indefinitely.' We had no idea when he would be able to return.

> Survival #3: Keep yourself busy. I am a 'To-do – list person' with most things in life anyway. It doesn't always mean I will get everything completed in the two week swing he's away, but it keeps my mind busy.

Pulling the car up to the drop off bay at Melbourne airport was eerie enough with no one blasting their horns at one another, taxis cutting everyone off ... not even a tumble weed in sight, but as soon as I witnessed Luke putting on his backpack, my eyes instantly filled and then poured out a lifetime of tears.

I can only describe it as what I believe it would feel like to drop off your loved one as they headed to war.

The feeling of the unknown ...

I knew that he would be safe, but when would I even physically see my fiancé again? Overreaction? Maybe, but with everything that had happened up to this point (and what was coming, I don't think I was).

The drive home from the airport, was a long empty freeway. The roads should have been full of cars, road rage and car sing-a-longs, instead, it was like driving all alone on a deserted road in the country, which made it easy to pull off into the emergency lane and cry a little more.

Misconception #1: 'Aren't you worried he will cheat?'

In a matter of two weeks, I had lost my birthday, our wedding and honeymoon, hens' day, my jobs (including a personal business) and now my fiancé ... it was my rock bottom.

The days merged into one, bottles of wine just didn't do it anymore, my hours outside my house were no longer bringing a smile to my face. I missed my human. I missed my family and friends (as no one was within the 5km legal radius). I missed working. I missed having a purpose and a reason for getting out of bed.

I tried my best to stay positive through our phone calls together. I knew that Luke was doing it tough too (especially at the start with two weeks isolation in a hotel room without even an open window), but I was crumbling.

I hurt. I was lonely, and the only reason I had for getting out of bed each day was to stop the cat annoyingly meowing and scratching on doors and furniture.

Luke and I had loosely discussed that after we returned from our Hawaiian honeymoon, we would look for a new home in

WA (either building or buying), and to start off our new chapter as husband and wife in a new state.

Fast forward a few more months (end of June 2020), I was finally allowed to enter the state. This was after spending hours searching for a rental home (as no one was wanting to accept a tenant application of two Victorians), and then once finding a new home, having to wait weeks to be allowed into Western Australia, and this was only with the help of an employer letter from Luke's work.

Australia became so divided during the pandemic, and coming from the East Coast to the West made me feel like an illegal immigrant being smuggled across the border.

I had four weeks to pack up our memories, possessions (including cars and the cat), find a removalist, book a flight and move. Definitely not the way Luke and I had planned starting our new chapter together as Mr. & Mrs.

I didn't really get to say goodbye to any of my friends and family, though I did get to spend a few days at my parent's house, which helped a little. Then came the anxiety and terror in starting again. I managed to kill my stress ball on the flight over, the poor lady sitting in front of me was covered in stress ball insides!

Finally, I'm here – living in Western Australia.

I'm in the same time zone at least.

Misconception #2: 'You must love all the alone time?'

Has it been easy? It has been easier in our relationship – but not in life.

Starting in a brand-new area in your late thirties, is as enjoyable as stabbing a fork into your eye.

Anxiety rolls in quicker than a tidal wave.

I needed to meet new people, find a job, discover a new favorite coffee shop and figure out why West Australians indicate when driving straight through a roundabout.

Luke and I were ready to start – again. Grab the bull by its horns so to speak, take fate into our own hands.

So November 2020, we decided that 2021 would be our year (we picked January 2nd, 2.1.21), and that we would start the year off with a positive, the biggest moment of our lives; we decided to elope, as we just didn't know when our Bali wedding could take place.

It was our couple secret (only a handful of people knew who helped us to organise the day), and it brought some positiveness back into our lives.

When Victorian borders opened back up, we naturally wanted our parents and siblings with us to share in our day (again), excitedly our parents booked their flights over and we started looking forward to the best way of starting 2021.

Misconception #3: 'He must be raking it in!'

… But we got to experience one last swing from our good luck fairy …

Borders closed AGAIN.

Luke's parents had made it over, but then on day two of their holiday, were forced to quarantine for another twelve days with us. And my parents never made it out of Victoria. I cried myself to sleep on New Year's Eve. I didn't even make it close to midnight, it wasn't the way I thought I'd be seeing out 2020 or in a new state with my fiancé …

However, our day was magical. Words cannot describe how I felt walking up the stairs in Cottesloe, and seeing my human's smile spread across his face. It was just me and him, and three of our friends, leaving behind everything that the world had thrown at us the last two-and-a-half years.

We have had so much go against us, defy us, try us and destroy us, and test us on every level.

Numerous people question me if my relationship with Luke is worth it, considering that he is 'never around.'

I've said it once, and I'll say it a million times – Luke is my favourite human.

We've experienced everything we've been told that can ruin a couple. We've been financially challenged, going through two years of planning and the process of building a house, only to lose it. We've had a long distance relationship, and long periods of separation, even while planning a wedding. In our case, our elopement was plan 'H'! But here we are, coming up to five years together, and we are (finally) happily married.

Being a FIFO wife was something I never even knew existed, yet something that would form to be a big part of my life.

Has it changed me? Absofreakinlutely!

It has made me stronger; it has made me more appreciative of everything in my relationship, especially when you calculate the time we have actually spent physically together.

Does it test you? YES!

Like when it's day three at home, and he does something to really tick you off and all you can respond with is, 'When are you going back to site?'

I don't believe a FIFO relationship works just because of a strong relationship. Sure it freaking helps – especially when it's a West and East Coast one, but what it really takes is two strong, reliable, trusting, faithful, honest individuals who believe in one another, who believe that their person is the ant's pants and will stop at nothing to make the world, and life, better for the other person.

It's sacrificing the everyday things most couples take for granted.

When you find your person, your favourite human – you will do anything to make it work – including packing up and moving to the other side of Australia.

'PERSONAL GROWTH AND HONEST CONVERSATION ON BOTH SIDES ARE THE ONLY WAY THROUGH. IT DOESN'T GET EASIER, YOU BOTH NEED TO CONTINUALLY WORK ON GETTING BETTER - TO GET BETTER AT ADAPTING, TO GET BETTER AT TALKING, TO GET BETTER AT TRUSTING. NONE OF THIS HAPPENS OVER NIGHT!'

Sheleila D'Paiva – 'The 'My Bad' Wife'

THE 'MY BAD' WIFE

NAME: SHELEILA D'PAIVA
INDUSTRY: MINING
RELATIONSHIP STATUS: DE FACTO
TIME IN INDUSTRY: 2 YEARS

First and foremost, I am not (yet) a wife. I'm sticking it out for this title though. ☺

We first met on Bumble in September 2018. We were a year into our relationship when he decided to make his career change away from the full-time family business as an electrician, which he had been doing since he was a teen, to FIFO for a mining company.

At this point, we weren't living together but were in the 'honeymoon' period of spending every night together at one of our places and still learning about each other. We had a bit of a challenging first year due to a health issue in the first few months, but we got past it and were in a pretty good place.

'I'm super independent, I'll be fine!' I remember thinking when he told me he was applying for a FIFO role; a 7:7 (7 days on, 7 days off) roster. I knew the reason he was moving away from contract work was to have more work-life balance. At the time, he was working six or seven days a week and wasn't getting enough time to spend with his new 'girlfriend' (me hehe), and see his friends and family, and doing all the things he loved - building his boat, being on his other boat, fishing, diving, re-arranging tools in one of his multiple sheds. This was always a lot to cram into a Saturday night and Sunday. Many of his friends were already FIFO. My Mum and her now-husband worked FIFO and my brother does too. I was used to celebrating birthdays early or late, or Christmas a week before or after. I knew the sacrifices that needed to be made to make it work. I got it. I understood the appeal and before meeting him, had even thought about FIFO roles in finance myself - more time and money are the two things everyone wishes they had more of besides good health. So, I was supportive.

Survival #1: Selfies - send pictures or videos all. the. time.

It was only a week on and week off after all and I wasn't the kind of person to tell someone what they should or shouldn't do in their career.

I asked a few friends whose partners were in FIFO for advice, but realised pretty quickly that the transition into FIFO for a new relationship was going to be different from their experiences, because FIFO was the only thing they had known for their entire relationship. I had also been single for four years, so I felt there was a whole different layer to add as well, I was still learning about him and how to be in a relationship, let alone a FIFO one - a whole different ball game.

The first morning he flew out, I dropped him to the airport and drove back to my apartment, where the only thing I had of his was a shirt he left me with his cologne sprayed on it. I put on his shirt but I still felt him missing. It was like my body thought we were no longer together, it instantly disconnected. My mind and the more logical side of me knew though that he was only going to work and he would be back ... in a short seven days.

I would later find out this was due to my body holding onto unprocessed childhood trauma even though I wasn't consciously aware of it.

> **Survival #2: There is no right or wrong in this game, do what works well for you *tweak as required.**

One thing I learnt, NOT so quickly, was that I needed a filter while he was away (at the very least), something I still need to work on. I'm pretty sure that first week I told him I felt single and in the first few months I told him I understood why people cheat. NOT nice to hear, I know. NOT that I agreed with it or that I would do it, but being used to your favourite person sleeping next to you every night, and their presence and support on a day-to-day basis, being gone - it can feel empty and lonely. It felt like a part of me was missing.

Let me clarify though, I am a busy woman and enjoy time by myself. I didn't feel I was codependent or needed him to make me happy. I strongly believe in the importance of keeping independence whilst being in a relationship (though, to be honest, maybe too much so), and having hobbies and interests. I work full-time in corporate, I write, I read, I gym, I dance, I paint, I draw, I have a beautifully large group of friends and of course my family, yet those seven days still went ever so slowly.

And oh, the things I kept telling myself to stay 'positive':

'It's only seven days, he will be back next week, it will be fine.'

'One week is nothing compared to three or four that other couples do.'

'It will be great to focus on myself and do things that I love more.'

'I'll have a week on, week off with my friends.'

'I'm used to being the third wheel.'

'I'm used to rocking up solo to events.'

Reading this back to myself now, I was serving myself a plate of toxic positivity and not validating or accepting my feelings or giving myself credit for the change we were experiencing. Maybe if I had been kinder to myself from the beginning we would have found our 'new normal' faster than we did, but I kept forcing myself to act and be a certain way.

Days went fast but nights always went slow, no matter how much I had to do.

I moved into his place by the end of 2019 thinking it would bring some comfort and ease, instead of driving to each other's houses and staying in different places. While there were some new comforts, like having all of his things and sleeping in our bed that we bought together, it also came with challenges. I moved in with him and his housemates after living alone for a few years, much further away from the city and where I worked and what I was used to. I moved into a much older and bigger house, one bedroom to five bedrooms. It was terrifying when I was home alone at night. It was quite a transition and I hated fly-out day because I didn't want to be in his unfamiliar house without him.

Survival #3: First and foremost, don't disconnect!

I found third-wheeling wasn't so fun when you've experienced being a balanced fourth wheel and rocking up to events solo when you finally have your person to drag to everything. It honestly sucked. I didn't realise at the time that I was putting pressure on him as well, mentally preparing that his weekends back were for me - God forbid he made plans to see his friends on weekends or chose his friends' events over mine, or even do something without me. Fair to say, it continued to get worse before it got better (which it is now, so hang in there).

I always cried to him the night before fly-out day, which is a Tuesday, but I often cried by about Sunday night again. It was a mixture of not enjoying where I lived without him but also openly sharing my emotions with him. I didn't share this with many others though because I knew how independent my friends thought I was.

'You'll get used to it.'

'I'm surprised, you're so busy.'

'It can't be that bad, it's only a week.'

I was independent. But I didn't get used to it. While their words were to be of support, it made me feel like I wasn't doing it right, doubting myself and our relationship. Maybe I wasn't the right person to be with someone who was FIFO. Maybe I wasn't strong enough for it or emotionally capable.

Misconception #1: Everyone is having affairs/cheating.

On top of the expectation that I should have been dealing with it better, there were the unsolicited comments I would get (all the time):

'Did you hear about those site wives though?'

'You know if they leave money in the freezer, the cleaners come back at night for some extra work?'

'Did you hear about x leaving y and the kids because he met her on site?'

'You know z cheated with someone on site?'

'They have these site lives they keep secret.'

'Everyone hooks up on site and then acts like they don't even know each other once they get on the flight back home.'

'You might trust him, but it's the girls up there you have to watch out for.'

Seeds on seeds on seeds, planted deep.

The amount of 'I've heard' and the 'be carefuls' would make the strongest of women doubt.

I very quickly texted him telling him NOT to leave money in the freezer by accident, something that (I think) we both can chuckle about now.

Misconception #2: Everyone drinks, so 'you have to drink'.

I remember one time he made a joke about having a site wife in front of his work colleagues and everyone laughed … except … me. That was a great time and he's not done it again!

Twisted within all these new insecurities was the unhealed childhood trauma of my parents divorcing, something I thought that had squared away in a neat little box inside me with little to no impact. Boy was I wrong.

The more vulnerable I was in the relationship, the more issues arised. I realised the physical act of him flying to work was triggering my insecurity of someone I loved leaving me. The unhealed child inside me, and the reason I stayed single for such a long time, was because I linked men to pain and a limiting belief that men will always, and inevitably, leave. And there he was, quite literally flying away.

I subconsciously started fights the night before fly-out day. I would flat out disconnect myself if the smallest thing made me unhappy. I found myself having panic attacks (which I have not had since I was a child), while he was away. I would very quickly and very easily go into fight or flight mode.

We were going around in a vicious cycle, by no fault of his, and we had to brainstorm different ideas on how to move forward because it was clearly unsustainable.

I have since seen a psychologist to work through my childhood trauma and highly recommend it, because even though I can't rewrite my history, we have been able to better understand my triggers and remove negative thought patterns. I also removed synthetic hormones from my body (contraception/Implanon) that I have continuously had for about nine years. I believe this was playing a role in being hyper-emotional during my cycle. We have also seen a counsellor together to give us the tools we can use when there is conflict. This has done wonders for us.

It's been just under two years since he's been FIFO, and what a ride it's been.

I can honestly say we've overcome most of the obstacles we've been faced with, no longer coming from a place of fear and insecurity, or pressing each other's buttons.

I've completely scrapped the toxic positivity and invalidating my feelings. If I feel sad, I allow myself to feel sad and I will tell him - no fake masks over here. I don't compare myself to anyone else's FIFO relationships or their story, and I trust in what we have and where we are going.

The housemates moved out and I repainted the downstairs area, bought pieces of art and plants to make the house more homely; it finally feels safe for me.

It's taken some time to get into the flow of FIFO life but we know what works for us now; daily calls (even if it's five minutes), text messages and random videos throughout the week.

Our daily non-negotiable when he is away is saying goodnight on the phone to each other every night. It doesn't have to be a long chat, just five minutes before bed, but I feel it makes all the difference.

We also make sure that we do some kind of activity when he is home. We are currently trialling fly-in day being date night, so we can go out to dinner together and aren't stuck cooking and cleaning. It's a chore-free night where we can just enjoy each other's company.

There are a few joys of him being away as well, that I like to focus on:

- having a clean house and being able to walk around barefoot for the time he's away (my week of no sand in the house is absolute bliss)

- cleaning while he is not around

- one-on-one time with the fur babies

- picking what I want to watch on Netflix without someone telling me it looks horrible

- not having to cook fresh dinners every night (his thing, not mine, I like to meal prep)

- the extra money that has been able to enhance our lifestyle and enlarge our goals (key!!!)

- the time for holidays we are now able to take

- the weekends away to visit my family

- the ridiculous amount of trust and communication we've had to develop in our short time together

- the mini reset button we get to press each time he flies in

- me time.

And then, of course, there is the first smile after a swing, the first hug I force onto him in the car even though he hates the awkward sideways hug, and the first kiss over and over again …

I wanted to share this story to show different complexities and layers that I never thought of when I first considered being in a FIFO relationship, even though I have a FIFO family, and nothing could have prepared me for it.

Misconception #3: Difficult to stay healthy on site.

Prior to being in a relationship, I had done a lot of work on myself, but the real work started when I was in relationship that I was ready to be vulnerable in and work on.

FIFO catapulted my own personal growth, but also that of our relationship, and whilst there were ups and downs, we were able to overcome the challenges and are more trusting and comfortable than we have ever been with each other.

And this was all in the first three years of our relationship … wish us well for the rest of it please!

Who knows how long he will be FIFO, maybe until we hit a few financial goals, maybe when we have kids or maybe this will be our forever lifestyle. But I hope sharing the transition, the challenges and how we overcame them will help other couples through their journey.

'Behind every happy couple lies two people who have fought hard to overcome all obstacles and interferences to be that way. Why? Because it's what they wanted' - Kim George.

'MINING HAS GIVEN OUR FAMILY A GOOD LIFE; IT IS NOT FOR EVERYONE AND NOT EVERYONE UNDERSTANDS THE SACRIFICES THAT ARE MADE BY THE PARTNERS/WIVES WHO STAY AT HOME TO HOLD THE FORT. YES FIFO IS HARD ON RELATIONSHIPS, BUT LIKE ANY RELATIONSHIP ... WHEN THERE IS A COMMITMENT TO MAKING IT WORK, IT WILL WORK. IT IS ABOUT THE COMMITMENT, SEEING WHAT IS GOOD AND KNOWING THE DESIRED OUTCOME.'

Ruth Walker – 'The Steadfast Wife'

THE STEADFAST WIFE

NAME: RUTH WALKER
INDUSTRY: UNDERGROUND MINING
RELATIONSHIP STATUS: MARRIED
TIME IN INDUSTRY: 1990-2021 WITH SOME BREAKS IN BETWEEN

The mining industry was not a planned choice but an opportunity that presented itself at the right time. Neither Luke nor I came from a background in mining of any sort. Luke had been a prawn fisherman for nine years and was used to living at work for long periods of time. Me, I never wanted to be a single mum and yet in a way, that is what parenting feels like at times in a FIFO relationship, although it has the bonus of having the full and constant support from the spouse. In the beginning, mobile phones were an absolute luxury, and we did not have a landline, so in reality it felt like being on my own and juggling the intentional sharing of responsibilities, ensuring Luke felt he had a place and responsibility when he was home. Though when at work, it's important that he is able to give his full attention, because hell, he needs to focus on safety while there.

You know, it is hard for me to remember what it was like in the first few years, but some memories have stuck. In 1989, we purchased land in Dongara, a small fishing town 400 kilometres north of Perth. It was the second time we applied for a loan from a bank and the application was based on both our incomes. I was eight months pregnant, and the bank representative could see I wasn't going to work much longer, so I am grateful to him for approving our application. We had a strong deposit, but the interest rates were at their highest and land prices had risen sharply the year before. We purchased a five-metre caravan, installed it on our forty acres, with an outdoor non-flush dunny, and were hoping to build our house, eventually. All our savings were invested in the purchase of the land, the small caravan and a sturdy Hilux ute.

My family was in Switzerland and Luke's family lived in Perth. I had some visits from my family over the years and Luke's visited occasionally; they were a bit sad to see us move so far away. As it turned out, it was good for us to be at a distance because I realised shortly into our marriage that Luke's father was verbally and emotionally abusive. After giving birth to our son, Luke went back to his employment of prawn fishing so he could earn a chunk of money. It was hard to get out of the rental cycle and become homeowners, as neither of us had education to earn high incomes.

Survival #1: Make a space for the partner in the family when he is home and fill it when he is absent.

We became parents to our beautiful son in April 1989, and in June we moved to our block of land. We lived in the caravan without running water or electricity. We set it up with an annex and a gaslight; it was quite cosy, even romantic - if you were on a holiday! We had a generator and carted water from town in a forty-four-gallon drum. We were trying to establish ourselves on the land and with local employment. We both had experience in all sorts of jobs, so there were some options available. Luke first found shift work for an export hay company, and after getting tired of working nights he found employment in the local cray-fish factory, also shift work. When Luke started working, our next-door neighbour drilled a bore for us in return for a couple of days' labour. We bought the bore casing and pump and a second-hand tank. It made life so much easier to now have water freely available. However, this new responsibility of keeping the tank full by starting up the generator, and not letting it overflow, made me very aware of water economy.

Survival #2: Help your partner be successful in his role in the family.

While Luke was working at the local crayfish factory, one of the ladies said to Luke that Golden Grove Minesite was looking for miners. Although Luke said he had no mining experience, she told him this was exactly what they were looking for; they wanted to train their own workers. Luke applied and was offered a position. This was back in 1990, when our baby was eighteen months old. I really didn't know much about the mining industry when Luke said he was going to apply. He was surprised to be contacted and excited to get an interview, but I had no idea what we were in for. The company interviewed me on their final interview to ensure this was going to be a long-term commitment from both parties. Luke was to fly from Geraldton to Golden Grove and so the 2:1 cycle began. The first great change was that regular money was coming in. The pay was a lot better than the shift work or the hourly rate at the crayfish factory.

This is how our FIFO life started when FIFO was not even a term. Luke has worked FIFO for many years. He trained on the different machines and eventually passed his shift boss ticket; there were breaks yes, but it was constant employment, well paid and offered comfort and security for me, so I could be a stay-at-home mum. Luke and I had decided that this was best, neither of us wanted to put our kids into day care. Luke gave me the responsibility of budgeting the money and sourcing things for our hobby farm, and eventually our house.

Survival #3: Give him time to adjust when he comes home.

My weeks were very busy as I ran the hobby farm and the business of building our house. I am an entrepreneur at heart, and open to fresh opportunities to add to our income, so we cultivated a veggie patch and planted fruit trees. We had chickens and a couple of sheep. There was plenty of physical work. We had no computers for the first few years, so most of my time was spent outdoors and caring for my son and later, two daughters. On Luke's roster off he was able to build the small house we had planned. It was nothing fancy but was able to get us out of the caravan. It was built with recycled materials and had one bedroom, bathroom, toilet and kitchen; later we added a lounge which was also the girls' bedroom while our son had the freshly converted caravan as his bedroom. It took us another ten years to build the main house. Luckily, we did not know that at the time, so we enjoyed all our wins and accomplishments.

It was hard to be on my own for two-thirds of the time, with Luke home for the other third. The nights were long and the children often missed their dad, so I was pacifying them when they were longing for daddy. I planned fun outings and special time for when dad was home and the children were always excited to see him. The cycle for me meant I was able to gracefully make room for husband and father when he came home. Really, that was my most important function. When Luke was at work, he had to give his all because he was responsible for the safety of his crew, and he took this responsibility very seriously. Although we were in some contact, he was unable to project himself fully into home life and give me his undivided attention as he was in a different world while at work. Normally it would take him a day to readjust when he came home. This meant I had to hold my urgent requests until the right moment. He would normally tell me when he was ready. I'm sure it was hard for him to go from work to home to work and adjust himself each time with shifts, food and society.

Misconception #1: 'FIFO workers have easy money.'

Another important responsibility I adopted was to plan Luke's week off so that when he was home the children had special time; fun-time, outings, picnics and holidays. It meant that Luke did not have to think about his role or his responsibility. He could slide into it with a little prompt here and there and be confident at it. I was the discipliner, the one who laid down the rules, made up the chore sheets so there was order and room for play. At Luke's 'last round birthday' the children shared their memory of dad to the guests and they all saw their childhood as fun when dad was home; dad played games, dad took them for outings and dad picked them up and dropped them off.

Romance was also very important. After two weeks at work each night at home was like a honeymoon. We were, and are still, very much in love. I hated it when we had disagreements. I felt like I was wasting precious time together. It was important that Luke left on a good and happy note, so all issues were resolved as quickly as possible. This was sometimes hard. It often meant I could not fully explore my anger, my disagreement, my sulkiness, my selfish needs and whatever else I wanted to persist in while in an argument. However, I learnt to listen, negotiate and find solutions that worked for us and was good for the well-being of the family. I would usually take some time out for myself and just go and do something for me. I needed a break from the 'round the clock responsibility' I had while he was away at work.

Misconception #2: 'FIFO wives like when their husbands go away.'

Once I got used to the FIFO cycle, I enjoyed the security, income and rhythm this provided. As the children started school, I also found odd jobs; cleaning, babysitting, factory work etc. in town. The income I earned was for luxuries for myself and travelling backwards and forwards to see my family in Switzerland once every three or four years. I took one of the children with me on each trip and they all love travelling now.

As a newly married woman, a new mother, and new to a small town, I made different friends. I had a few single mums as friends for the two weeks Luke was at work. They understood and accepted that for one week out of three I was unavailable. I also had 'couple' friends, who I noticed were reacting to me with caution when Luke was at work. Some of the women saw me as a possible threat while Luke was not around. You know, this could well have been an imagined notion I picked up, but being emotionally intelligent, I knew that I was not as welcome on my own as I was with Luke. Luke had less interest in my single mum friends, as for him, socialising was more about getting to know other families and making male friends who shared his interest of cars, building and gadgets. He is a devoted husband and I have always trusted him completely. For religious reasons he never drank alcohol or smoked, a choice we made shortly after our son was born. The money we saved no longer smoking or drinking we used to travel, camp and have farm toys.

One of the comments I often heard from family and friends was, 'I don't know how you can let your husband go to work in a mine.' I received this comment more often than I care to count. Sometimes it hurt deeply, like an accusation, a cut, as if it were me who sent him down the hole because I was a money-hungry bitch. As if I made him go to work because I needed the money. The thing is, I probably would have taken responsibility for this comment, had it been true, if I really did use his money for my selfish needs. To be honest, after we paid the government their share and purchased another item for the building of the house there was just enough left over for our necessities. I often thought my single mum friends had more money from the government than I did with my husband working his arse off and me growing vegetables and living in a caravan. It was tough setting up house from zero. We purchased every tool, nail, power tool, piece of wood, fence post, water pipe and the list could go on for a long time.

A traumatic experience was the time I was in my third pregnancy and I started to bleed. We were in the granny flat in 1993 with the outdoor dunny, as no septics were installed at that time. It is hard to imagine a time before mobile phones or internet access now, but we had neither. The bleeding and cramping started during the night and I had to go to the dark outdoor dunny. I am not exactly sure what happened, but I know I was there for some time cramping like crazy and bleeding. I cared for myself as best as I could till morning. I was losing what seemed to be a lot of blood. I was getting dizzy, and knew I could not drive myself and my two young children to the hospital, but I also knew I needed to get there. I ended up calling on my neighbour to see if he could drive me, which he did. I was put under anaesthetic and the gynaecologist told me later that the foetus was no longer in my womb and he ensured that the placenta had dispatched fully so there would be no infection. Luke was able to come home early. He came to the hospital and took me home. My good friend took my children to her house and cared for them while I was not there. The worst thing about the experience was the loss of life and the lack of grieving over miscarriages. I had another baby two years later.

Around 1994 we had finally built our small house and a septic system, a bigger and newer water tank and were beginning to 'get on our feet.' It was then we figured we were paying too much tax and looked for ways to reduce the amount of tax we paid. It so happened that Luke's parents could no longer stay in their property with an acre of land on a steep slope. The discussion rose around their need to move out of their house into a smaller unit or townhouse perhaps. We discussed with them our thoughts of an investment property and they decided to accept our offer, with some conditions. The following conditions should paint a picture. They wanted to choose the property; they picked a two-story townhouse with two bathrooms and three toilets in Yokine. The property was being built. It had become fashionable to sub-divide town blocks into three townhouses, perhaps still a novel idea then, and these properties had risen in price. Luke's parents told us how much rent they 'could' pay, they needed the house completed with insulation, blinds and garden. Our accountant thought it would be a good investment and tax deduction for us and in a way it was. However, with this financial situation, the building of our own house slowed right down. Three years later, my parents-in-law were visiting us in our little one bedroom flat with three young children. The men were outside on a project while I was bathing my baby in the kitchen sink. Grandma liked to talk and saw herself as a blessed soul from the upper socio-economic bracket. She was telling me how difficult it was living in her air-conditioned spacious town house. Suddenly I realised she was never going to thank us for making sacrifices on our home so she could live comfortably. I later talked to Luke and explained that I wanted to sell our town house investment property, as our finances didn't allow progress on our own building project. The parents quickly found somewhere else to rent and left us with a messy tenant while we tried to sell the house, in a now slow and depressed market. We were often told how uncaring we (I) were to kick them out of their house. Our relationship deteriorated dramatically. This was a lesson learned around family wanting to benefit from FIFO income without contributing in helpful ways.

Although there were long times of absence, the beauty of the FIFO life is when the 'presence' is twenty-four hours over a few days, in a child's life this feels like 'all the time.' FIFO is hard yes, but like any relationship, when there is a commitment to making it work, it can work. I have never liked my husband leaving for work or the time he was working away. From time to time he has tried to work locally, but as his training and experience is in the mining industry, he is completely undervalued and underpaid in other jobs. There have been breaks and he has worked in other industries, but when he had enough of the low wages, he would return to mining.

Misconception #3: 'FIFO wives are money-hungry.'

There were many lessons looking back; life lessons and specific FIFO lessons. For my part, I am grateful to the industry as it provided a steady income while the economy had its ups and downs. With FIFO we could stay in one place and the children could make good friends, and when it was time, we chose to move. FIFO allowed Luke to be a present dad and husband when he was off work and we enjoyed his time at home with us immensely. Luke appreciated what I did while he was away by giving me all his money to manage and trusting me fully in running the family business. There is not much I would change; life is good and I am grateful for all the time off.

'GREAT THINGS ARE ACHIEVED THROUGH LOTS OF LITTLE UNGLAMOROUS MOMENTS. SOMETIMES IT ISN'T THE WINS THAT SET YOU APART FROM EVERYONE ELSE. WE HAVE A SAYING IN OUR HOME, WHICH IS 'FAIL FORWARD!' OUR KIDS WILL TELL YOU, IT'S OKAY TO FAIL BECAUSE THAT'S WHERE THE LESSON IS. USE THAT LESSON TO GROW, MOVE FORWARD AND SUCCEED.'

Brook O'Brien – 'The Not So Glamorous Wife'

THE NOT SO GLAMOROUS WIFE

Name: Brook O'Brien
Industry: Drilling & Exploration
Relationship Status: As good as married :)
Time in Industry: 4 years

They call it the 7 pm train. You miss it, you're screwed! Our kids get on that train each and every night to visit the land of nod. Except every third week when our routine is completely thrown out the window. Why? We live the 'oh, so glamorous' FIFO life; my senior offsider husband (and man of the house), our humble eight-year-old son (also man of the house), and our delightful four-year-old daughter. What does this mean exactly, you may be wondering? It means, every third week is a party, to the under-nines and over-thirty-fives!

YIPEE, daddy's home!! Dinner, bed time, jobs, everything that keeps this ship afloat, sinks into an abyss of late nights, popcorn, nerf wars and junk food. This mumma, (hi, that's me and not quite thirty-six) takes this time, I call the 'third week,' to completely switch off! Although my hubby is not a clean-up, pack away, routine guru, he is pretty amazing in this way. He has never once complained about me using some of his week off to just sit and take a breather. He cooks delicious dinners every night and even attempts the school lunches. I'm certain if I wanted to sit on my ass the whole week, he would advocate for me. I'm not sure if it's his own guilt of working away that turns him into our very own Jamie Oliver, or the fact that I'm really not that great of a cook. Either way, it works in my favour and I am not ever going to complain!

But there is a catch … the catch is, that fourth week. That bloody week when he leaves is a complete and utter mess. I feel like I'm cleaning up and re-organising a house that has just held a community event and tightening the ropes of two mouthy teenagers. I know our intentions are for him to leave with our shit together but honestly, I feel overwhelmed. That is, until the following week when all order re-enters our household once again. To get there however, requires me to do a whole lot of house work and nagging, and it is here my guilt kicks in, and I promise myself that I will stay on top of things next swing, which I know isn't true. Going from a plus one to a minus one, means regardless of how hard you try, things are not going to be smooth sailing and no consistent routine is ever going to hold up solid. So then I remind myself to just ride the wave, which brings me to the fifth week where normality shows itself. And, the cycle continues.

> Survival #1: Communication and transparency. Common sense, right? But this is probably the same reason so many FIFO relationships fail. If your communication is solid, you're already on top and if it isn't, work on it!

Why did we enter the FIFO life? I have asked myself that same question more times than I can count. In all honesty, it came down to time and money. We envisioned a mum for our children who could work less. A mum who could do drop-offs and pick-ups, and at the same time be present with our toddler and little boy. I went back to work when my son was six months old, and I cringed at the thought of doing that a second time. After experiencing motherhood and life, we knew if I could be the one to devote the early years to our children, we were going to make it happen. My husband could also be there with us for more than just the weekends. In addition, we were sending our son to a school with a hefty price tag. My husband worked a nine-to-five job that just wasn't cutting it. We also had a small tax debt, due to my husband's work requiring him to be on ABN and his great mathematician skills. In other words, we were broke and up shit creek without a paddle. I remember having to postpone our mortgage for a month. A bank manager looked at our earnings and spending and in shock said, 'Wow, your wages can't cover what you need to spend.' I felt like saying 'No shit,' but I took a deep breath and gave a little giggle! To our credit we were always ahead in repayments, and somehow throughout this entire journey, we have managed to never go without, except for toilet paper on the odd occasion. Regardless, my strong desire to postpone going back to work, and my husband's desire to expand his own opportunities within the workforce, encouraged us to take the leap. And did I mention we were broke? It seemed like a no-brainer. We made a pact we would make every moment count and were feeling pretty self-assured we were onto a good thing. My husband had worked away when my son was a toddler, so we were already pros! We had even made the monkey homemade videos for me to play while dad was away. We would obviously keep doing this throughout our FIFO journey. No worries, right?! Let's fast forward to last night, when my daughter asks, 'Excuse me daddy, but why do you always call me when I am already in bed?' Daddy did not reply, 'Oh I am sorry sweetheart, I will have to make you another one of my videos.' ☺

Looking back now I have to laugh, because throughout this journey so much has changed. I probably have more on my plate than ever. Our kids go to an amazing government school and time … there is never enough time! Some of the reasons we took on FIFO life are still some of our biggest struggles. When I hear of new FIFO families who share every spare moment FaceTiming on messenger, I sometimes wonder if they too will succumb to it all, becoming immune to the lifestyle, and masters at playing phone tag. I was recently speaking to a dear friend whose husband had just begun FIFO and my heart was warmed at how connected they still were. The chaos hasn't hit them yet, and I hope and pray it never does.

> Survival #2: Connect. Take time out to spend with each other but also connect with other FIFO mums and families. Share dinners together, spend family time together and make connections that run deep. Enjoy the journey together. Be around those who make you happy and encourage you.

Chaos! Remember that week, the one where my partner departs and leaves me with an array of mess; the week I find myself yelling a whole lot more and hating myself for it. I am a little lost. Feeling failure, at something I once thought was a piece of cake. Parenting is life-changing, exuberating and a whole lot easier when you have the energy and someone to share it with. I struggled to live in the moment, something I felt so natural with before. That scared the crap out of me and it sometimes still does. It's a constant juggling act and the kids can sometimes get less of you rather than more. Our pact to make every moment count was no longer being executed as easily as we imagined. So, my plate was full, my happiness was falling, and my life was lived in fortnights. I was scared my fatigue and burn-out was going to impact our kids and it pushed me into a downward spiral. I had tiny little beings I was nurturing, and I wanted to get it all 'right.' Us mums put so much pressure on ourselves to be amazing, without realising we already are. It was my biggest downfall. Time, self-growth and some truly WONDERFUL friends have helped me to realise this, but the pressure I put upon myself was debilitating. I won't lie; Lexapro was my sidekick for a few months. Anti-depressants were touched, fights were had, doors were slammed! When they say women are from Venus and men are from Mars, this is never more true than when you live the FIFO life. There is an expectation that women can keep everything afloat, alone, burnt-out, with no breaks AT ALL. The men are meant to just hang out in isolation for two weeks, and then slip back into the mix of family life. It's bloody hard! I thank my friends who were there for me, who packed my kids snacks, treated them like their own and unknowingly helped me out when I was at my lowest. I hope they know who they are and that I will be forever grateful. They understood me when my husband did not.

> Survival #3: Let go of perfection. I pictured what my life would look like and when it went south, I crumbled. Let there be tears, let there be mess, enjoy a Whopper three days a week if you have to. Allow yourself to ask for help. This is a big one for me. My friend constantly had an au pair. Her husband was FIFO and she had all her shit together, or so it seemed. She inspired me and took the shame out of asking for help. So for a good year, my cousin lived with us off and on and became our live-in au pair. I also had my aunty cook us meals for a while. Whatever works, do it! Your happiness, energy and mental state should come before all else.

My husband did not understand why we NEEDED early dinners, magnesium baths, probiotics, 7 pm trains and no TV before bedtime. It was so this FIFO mum could grip her cup of tea (sanity) and sit with Friends (the TV show), all before she herself slipped between the sheets to start the day again. And I did not understand why he couldn't call us at a reasonable hour or be more energetic when he did. So beware FIFO dads, when you call the kids past their bedtime, mumma bear is not going to be jumping with joy. I felt like he wanted me to roll out the red carpet when he got home and I detested it.

At the same time, we were planning holidays, trips, excursions, photos, trying to squash memories into our kiddies' hippocampus, to make up for all the missed milestones and misunderstandings. It was chaos!! So what did I do, I did what every sane mother would do and added more to my plate. I watched parenting blogs, read books and encouraged my better half to do the same. I upskilled my family in resiliency, learnt about music and frequency through Tenille Bentley (I mention her name because she is by far one of the most transformational ladies I have met), and took meditation classes, in hope of finding the answer on how to best manage the FIFO life. As much as these things impacted our family positively, there is no magic answer; only trial and error and the power of transparency.

> Misconception #1: Having a FIFO husband is like being a single mum. I have a lot of respect for single mums and definitely a greater respect over the last few years, but the two can't be compared. Having someone come and go all the time brings a different type of instability into the household, but it was also a joint decision and we are very much partners in it all.

FIFO will highlight any struggles or insecurities your relationship has, and if you don't have a solid foundation, expect there to be turbulence, and that life could get rocky. I am pretty confident when I say many FIFO relationships fail, and cracks become wide crevices. It's not a bed of roses and money injections, as some may believe. At times, it's a damn hard struggle. It is not just the women; the men struggle too. My husband struggled with isolation. If you are not a big drinker, you will need to become one, otherwise you're sitting in your room, alone, swing after swing, until you find your crew. Men aren't great at asking for help either. The man of our house was one of those men. He hit rock bottom, battling with the black dog. One day, he reached out and learnt not only was he dealing with isolation, he also was living with ADD. Abundantly Different and Happily Divine, as I now like to call it. My point being, in between FIFO life, is life; love, loss, birth, death, health, wealth, friction, depression, excitement, laughter, and memories. For us it was many of those things, sprinkled with a diagnosis of ADD.

> Misconception #2: You must be rolling in money. Oh how I wish! It all evens out. Usually one parent works less to compensate the other being away. Then there is that thing called tax. Money should not be the only reason why you choose the FIFO lifestyle.

As a FIFO couple, you may fight or figure something out, but then bam he is gone on a plane again and everything that has happened pauses for a fortnight. Road bumps can last weeks or even months. But now we had a reason why communication was tricky, depression was harder to navigate, and why the car rego wasn't paid. It was a new road for us, one we had to carefully navigate together. My husband felt like he had changed in some way; like he had to get to know himself again. I believe ADD is almost a super power. I needed to get him to see it through my eyes, because if he couldn't let the magic work in his favour, life would be a constant battlefield. The self-talk forcing him to believe he was no longer who he once was, was only magnified when sitting alone in a box, while getting accustomed to the serotonin inhibitors passing through his body, along with my lack of understanding as to why he wasn't reading every book and signing up to every course in his free time. That women are from Venus, men are from Mars stuff - it frustrated the hell out of me. He was drowning but wasn't reaching for a life boat.

If I can pass on any advice, it's to teach your sons how to express their emotions, encourage them to cry and listen when they ask for help, because this man was on the brink of defeat and if no one had reached out, well, my thoughts won't let me wander there. He later shared on social media how I got him through a tough time. But did I, in those fly-by weeks he was here? I am not convinced, but I do know he is liking who he is more and more, and the credit goes to him.

Is it worth it?

> Misconception #3: Us FIFO mums do nothing. We work full time raising children, we go to work ourselves, run the house and organise many busy schedules. Our partners are often not at home, and when things go wrong they are hundreds of kilometres away. We become skilled at the most random things, but it isn't at doing nothing.

I don't know? I'm so acclimatised to it now I'm unsure I would survive the alternative. Some days yes, others no. Did the FIFO life bring us closer? Yes. Did it pull us apart? Yes. Did we change? Yes. Will our relationship be what it was before FIFO? We sacrifice things in life to take leaps; leaps of faith that one day it will all pay off. Relationships evolve. It will never be the same, but it will be something new and we will navigate through it together.

I do know I am not as patient, kind, considerate or gentle as I once was. FIFO has built a strong exterior around me, that lets me just get the job done. To be honest, being that same, soft human would have only seen me crumble under immense pressure. My boundaries are stronger, and I am truly appreciative of the time we spend with those who create joy in our lives. At times, I wonder if he will one day tire of the person I am now, and at other times, I feel like I'm dealing with a third child. And then there are times we are a dynamic duo, the ideal team! They say love conquers all, but I say, ride the wave and see where life takes you. Keep growing, hopefully together, and let this journey create something new and even better. I believe your hardships eventually develop your strengths and I am truly blessed to give a voice to any FIFO family, to unleash some myths on our oh, so glamorous lifestyles!

I have vowed for 2021, I will stop feeling guilty. We live in a household where failure is welcome, and in turn, so is my own. This year we are taking chances, opening our doors to a new business; Perth Creative Party Hire, with women who have shared this FIFO journey with me. Get up and show up. What will be will be. There it is. FIFO life, the good the bad and the ugly. It's life and it will be as you create it. Remember to sprinkle gratitude along the way, and your journey will be so much more enjoyable. And if all else fails,

Just keep swimming.

With love B.

'FIFO WAS SOMETHING WE ALWAYS THOUGHT ABOUT AND WHEN A CHANCE OPPORTUNITY CAME KNOCKING, WE KNEW IT WAS TIME TO 'JUST DO IT.' I'VE ALWAYS BELIEVED THAT EVERYTHING HAPPENS FOR A REASON, AND IT FELT RIGHT. WAS IT DAUNTING NOT KNOWING WHERE WE WOULD END UP OR HOW WE WOULD MANAGE? YEP. WOULD I GO BACK AND CHANGE IT? ABSOLUTELY NOT. THE LIFESTYLE MAKES YOU STRONG, RESILIENT AND INDEPENDENT AND I KNOW I AM THE BEST VERSION OF MYSELF BECAUSE OF IT.'

Michelle Gaudieri – 'The Grateful Wife'

THE GRATEFUL WIFE

NAME: MICHELLE GAUDIERI
INDUSTRY: MINING
RELATIONSHIP STATUS: MARRIED
TIME IN INDUSTRY: 8 MONTHS

My FIFO journey started when I was young and we moved to the big city after growing up for the first few years of my life in the Pilbara. My dad met my mum back in Croatia and their married life began in the Pilbara. His first job was working on the railways, and from there his career thrived.

Four kids later, they decided it was time to move us all to the city and start the next chapter of our lives. That was when I was introduced to FIFO. From the moment we came to Perth, my dad was a FIFO dad, and that's all I ever knew. I remember crying every night before he would leave, and I would always draw him a picture to take with him. Thinking back now, I don't know when I stopped doing it, but as a parent myself, I can only imagine how much that would have broken his heart a little (insert crying face). But what I didn't realise at the time (well, I mean who would when you're an oblivious kid and then turn into an annoying attitude-filled teenager), was how much my mum played a huge significant role in making the FIFO life work for our family. I took it all for granted. She did everything for the four of us. My sisters are quite a few years older, so when dad was away, mum would work night shift while my sisters looked after me and my younger brother. It wasn't until I became a parent, even more so evident now as a FIFO wife and mum myself, that I realise the huge sacrifice both my parents made, to give me, my sisters and my brother, the life we have today. My mum and dad are my heroes, my everything, and most importantly, my inspiration.

My husband and I have two beautiful boys who are our everything. We've been together for over twelve years and grew together from young ones hitting up the night clubs every Saturday. Honestly I couldn't think of anything worse right now; our favourite nights are being at home with the boys. Okay, I mean, our favourite nights are when they are sleeping soundly and we can enjoy a vino while watching the latest Netflix series.

Survival #1: Never go to bed angry with your partner and finish any argument there and then. Talk, talk, talk.

I work part-time, and it's a bloody juggle, but I love it most days. I love the sense of accomplishment after a long day, finishing up with a clean house, putting the washing away, or cleaning the glass balustrades that breed fingerprints, all after dealing with school, toddler tantrums, and work woes. Ever since my husband and I got together, we always had the FIFO gig in the back of our minds for him. He was working as a tradesman, and I guess we both saw the benefit of FIFO from my dad, who was still very much in the game back then. He would apply for jobs, but nothing eventuated. Eventually, as time went on, we grew up a little, started focusing more on our future together as a family and he decided he wanted to follow his other dream which was running his own business. I supported his choice whole-heartedly and off on to the next path of our life we went.

Fast forward eight years and two beautiful boys, the business was well and truly up and running, and it was great. But it started getting busy, really busy. This meant he was coming home and spending all his time doing admin. He would get call-outs on weekends, and he was stressed. He is so hardworking that he never whined about it, but we both got to a point where we realised that maybe, we should consider the FIFO idea again. It was either grow the business (and likely grow the stress), or try FIFO. It is hard and daunting to decide to completely shut a business you've been building for eight years, especially as he was borderline ready to employ others due to the growth we were experiencing, but we made the decision together to see what would happen. So, a few months later there was a chance opportunity to jump into FIFO, and here we are, almost eight months later. Was the transition hard? Yes. I am not going to lie. Not only did we close the business and start the FIFO life, we also decided to sell our house and move, without anywhere to go. We ended up living at my parents for four months until we found our own place. It was a crazy six months for us; it was honestly an absolute blur. In the beginning, I felt like a fraudulent FIFO wife because I was literally living with my parents when my husband was away, so I didn't really feel the full brunt of it. It wasn't until we moved out into our own house that I really realised the shit we go through.

Survival #2: Sometimes, you need to close the door to the toy room rather than clean it, tomorrow is a new day!

In saying that though, we are lucky to have a village around us to help, and some days it feels like an entire town! It's the village around me, my people, our family and friends, who help me get through the days when my husband is away. I am so thankful I have help with school pickups and drop offs, babysitting, food shopping if I need it, and dinners made. You know, those things that might seem so little to others and just a part of everyday life, but when you are a FIFO wife and mum, it's the little things, like dinner being cooked, that change your entire night for the better. And with this I say, if you are blessed enough to have help around you, then please, I beg you, please don't be too proud to ask for help if you need it! Trust me, if you have one less thing to stress about, that turns into a little extra happiness, and sometimes that's all you need to seize the day, girlfriend.

> **Survival #3: Ensure that your cupboards are plenty stocked with coffee and vino so that you don't ever find yourself depleted of either when needed.**

Something that helps me, especially on those really shit days, is that no matter how shit the day has been, or how shit the whole week has been, I find something to be grateful for. And it's that mindset that gets me through. I have my moments; moments where nothing is going right. I'm defeated, I've made the fiftieth meal for my boys and they just. won't. eat. it (cue internal screaming), and I am just so goddamn frustrated with everything! It's those times I wish my husband was home with us, to take the edge off, to just let me have five minutes to refresh. Because let me tell you, there are days and nights when I absolutely resent the fact that my husband can go home after a day at work and have his meals cooked for him, jump into a nice quiet room and do whatever the hell he wants. And yes, I know its not easy for him in the sense he works long hours and swings, trust me, I know that, but there are certainly some days I wish I could swap, just for one night. I guess though, I am so grateful for everything, that I push through those moments and come out on the other side.

Gratitude is a huge part of my life, and something I practice daily. I'm grateful for literally everything; the air we breathe, our health, my boys, my family, my friends, my friends who are family, the food we get to eat, the roof over our heads, the green grass in our backyard, the air-conditioning in our house. Like I said, literally, everything. I saw the hard work my parents went through, moving to Australia from the other side of the world, with no ability to speak English and absolutely no family here, yet they worked damn hard to build the wonderful life I have, and now I get to continue to build on this life with our FIFO opportunity. All I can think is, 'how bloody lucky am I?' Together with my gratitude attitude, I am a huge believer and implementer of ROUTINE! Of course there will be times when routine goes completely out of the window, but I need to have some sense of control and stability in my life when home with the boys, and that's where routine comes in. It is in the little things like, dinner at the same time, followed by bath, then stories, then play - you know how it goes. Trust me when I say, if you can implement one bit of routine into your day, it will feel less manic. You know what to expect, your children know what to expect and then when your partner is home, they know what to expect and don't completely eff shit up when they're home, ha, happy days!

Misconception #1: You have so much money that you can literally do anything.

My husband is obviously the reason I am a FIFO wife and mum, but not is he only my husband, the FIFO worker, he is my soul mate, my best friend and most importantly, my team mate. We are a team. Always have been and always will be. We have each other's back, and that's something I find is paramount when you're in the FIFO game, especially with kids. We as the wives, girlfriends, partners etc. play a huge role in their career by being the ones who stay home and keep the ship sailing. So you could say, it's our career too. They might be the ones bringing in the fish, but we are the ones who stay on board and make sure as hell that ship stays afloat. And, do you know what is the most important key in not letting the ship completely sink to the bottom of the ocean? Communication. We talk, every day, and we talk about anything and everything.

As we started the FIFO journey, it was an understandably anxious time for me. I will preface this with the fact that my husband has never done anything for me to doubt his commitment to me, or our marriage and our boys. But my thoughts started going into overdrive; my mind and my imagination are my worst enemies. He was going away, to another place, where there would be other people, males but females also and it weirdly started playing on my mind. I am not usually an anxious person, but I certainly have moments where anxiety gets the better of me. I started delving into thoughts that he would be spending more time with these people, okay, more time with these girls, than with me. What if he fell in love with one of them? What if he connected so strongly with someone up there, that he decided he didn't want to be with me anymore? All the FIFO stories I had heard really began playing on my mind, and it was not a fun time. But instead of letting it fester away and continue to build into a huge thing that could have eventually imploded, I told him about it all. I told him about how I was feeling, why I was feeling this way and what it was making me think. Just by being able to do that made me feel so much better. It's not rocket science that communication is absolutey key in any team. For teams to work, you must communicate. So when starting this FIFO journey, and living through the initial effects it had on me, I realised that I needed to make sure we had the lines of communication open at all times, especially when he was away. I needed to remind myself that he is not a mind reader and if anything was going on in my head then I needed to tell him, and not expect him to figure it out. We talk almost every night. We never end a conversation on angry terms and we will finish any argument before we go to bed at night. But it's the talking, keeping him in the loop about what is going on with us back home, that keeps him feeling like he is still part of everything. It helps to bridge the gap of being away from the boys. Whilst it's hard for us at home to hold down the fort and keep the ship afloat, albeit with some turbulent waves, we need to remember that it's tough for him too. So, I make sure that I send all the photos and videos of the boys to him. I want to keep his spirits up while he is away. Our boys are our reason for embarking on the FIFO journey; to make a better life for them and sometimes he needs that reminder. When he is going through the grind of another twelve-hour day, and we hit the dreaded ten days into the swing, when you really bloody feel the time apart from each other, that one video of the boys saying hello makes his day and gives him the motivation to keep going until he is home.

Misconception #2: As the wife/mum you don't need to work, so why are you?

It's the time at home altogether as a family that drove us to start this journey. When my husband is home, he is home now. He isn't stressing about doing invoices, he isn't worrying about how he is going to get his work done. He is present with us. The shift in him since we started this journey has been very notice-able. When he was running his own business, he couldn't help but feel guilty if he wasn't working. But now, that guilt is gone, and without fail, every first morning he is back, he is ready to go and jump into the day with the boys. It's those moments that makes me realise this is all worth it. On the time is he is back, it's my opportunity to go do my things, such as hair appointments, shopping, catch-ups with my girlfriends, but I make sure there is balance. I don't rush out immediately and just leave him with the boys; it's not fair. Yes, I guess some might say it's not fair that I don't get to do any of that when I want when he is away, but it comes down to the fact that I want to spend time with him. We have set days on his time home that we spend together as a family and nothing else is ever planned on those days. We make sure, well try to make sure, that we have one date night/day when he's home that we remember us. At times it can be hard to juggle and fit it all in, because he has his family too, but for the most part, we make it work, and that's what matters.

So, there it is. All of that you've just read, is the reason why I am here today, a FIFO wife and mum. I almost feel like it was embedded in my genetics and I was bound for the FIFO lifestyle. And the genetics thing is backed by the fact both my sisters are FIFO wives and mums, AND my brother is a FIFO worker. I mean, stats right?! Don't get me wrong though, some nights, okay most nights, I am utterly exhausted and I just want to sloth on the couch and not move. There are days where I want to be me for a moment; no dishes, no washing, no vacuuming, no refereeing between two very boisterous boys, and I just want my husband home. But feeling that way only makes me human! It's okay if you feel that way too. At the end of the day, I remember how grateful I am for all the opportunities we now have, because we launched ourselves into the FIFO lifestyle. And honestly, I cannot see us going back to how we were before.

'TO BE TRAVELLING AUSTRALIA FULL-TIME WITH OUR LITTLE FAMILY IS A DREAM COME TRUE. TRAVELLING WHILE BEING A FIFO FAMILY ISN'T FOR EVERYBODY, BUT IT IS DEFINITELY FOR US. YOU WILL BE CHALLENGED IN A NEW WAY. YOU ARE WITHOUT YOUR SUPPORT SYSTEM IN A PLACE WHERE YOU USUALLY KNOW NOBODY, BUT THE TRAVELLING COMMUNITY IS A COMMUNITY THAT WE ARE SO LUCKY TO BE A PART OF. THEY LOOK OUT FOR EACH OTHER AND I'VE NEVER FELT SO SAFE. WE HAVE MADE MEMORIES THAT WILL LAST A LIFETIME.'

Rhianna Fazldeen – 'The Travelling Wife'

THE TRAVELLING WIFE

NAME: RHIANNA FAZLDEEN
INDUSTRY: OIL & GAS
RELATIONSHIP STATUS: MARRIED
TIME IN INDUSTRY: 18 YEARS

My husband Ben, myself and our two children are a travelling FIFO family! We travel Australia full-time in our twenty-one-foot caravan. Travelling while working FIFO isn't for everybody, but we think our country is too beautiful not to explore, our time is too valuable not to spend together and our children are too precious to have somebody else raise them in their early years. We explore some of our country's most beautiful beaches and remote locations. We love to chase sunsets and throw a line in every drop of water we can find. This is a glimpse into our life!

We both came from FIFO families, so it was a given that he would become a FIFO worker and I would marry one. Most of the males in my family work on oil rigs, and Ben has three older brothers in the industry. He is thirty-four now and been in the game for almost the entire eighteen years of his working life. We were both raised in country Queensland, a small town called Roma, which is the first place in Australia that natural gas was discovered. It is a hub for the oil and gas industry. We then moved to Toowoomba separately about eight years ago. While we knew of each other in Roma, and knew many of the same people, we didn't get together until we were living in Toowoomba.

A few years ago, when Jasmine, our daughter, was two, we trialled an 'in-town' job for twelve months. It was honestly the worst year of our relationship. I've never lived with a male full-time in my life. Coming from a FIFO family, and also having two serious relationships before Ben, who also worked FIFO, living day-in, and day-out with him was tough for me.

> **Survival #1: Appreciate each other's struggles. Things are tough for hubby out at work. But on the flipside things are tough for mum at home with the kids doing everything solo.**

He was gone before the sun was up. I was working full-time, and getting home at 6 pm most nights. He would collect Jasmine from day care, then I would get home, feed everybody, bath and bed, only to wake up in the morning and do it all over again. No treasured family time, no travelling; just work and no play. Weekends were spent exhausted, catching up on housework and yardwork, and a bit of arguing in there too. That's what happens when you're tired and stressed and barely know each other anymore. We trialled a separation during this time too, because we lost who we were. We likely would still be apart, but Ben's dad suddenly passed away which sadly was the thing that brought us back together and helped us re-evaluate things. This was when he made the decision to get back into the oil and gas industry.

On time off, we have always tried to do things together. We miss out on half of our life doing this job and don't like to sacrifice any time. I always tried to make sure we were up to date with the house and yardwork before he got home, but with having a house, there is always something to be done!

We always said 'one day' we would love to travel Australia, but never considered that we could do it while we were young with small kids. I ran into a girl I knew and she told me they were packing up their lives to go travelling Australia! 'Wow!' I said, 'I wish we could do that.' She replied with, 'Why can't you, what's stopping you?' and that's where our dream began.

I went home and told Ben about the conversation, not so subtly expressing my interest, and to my surprise he agreed it was something that he was keen to make happen as well. So, we started planning. We originally gave ourselves twelve months to get on the road, but we were so excited that within three months we couldn't help ourselves. We sold everything we owned besides a small storage container, with only our most sentimental and irreplaceable belongings, and before we knew it, we were living in our twenty-one-foot caravan!

We have been living full-time in our tiny home, exploring Australia for the last sixteen months. We have Jasmine, who is six and Finn who is two. Ben also has two older boys who join us on holidays. Ben works a two weeks on, two weeks off roster, and we find this swing to be perfect for travelling!

> Survival #2: Communicate about what you need. That maybe hubby needs a rest day when first coming home instead of jumping straight into dad mode. Also that wife is fucked from dealing with the kids for weeks with no help, and she may need extra help, or some time out to do something she wants to do.

Logistically, things can be a bit tough to navigate. Given that his point of hire is in Toowoomba, we fly him from wherever we are in the country, to Toowoomba to get him to work. We miss out on about half a day travelling each way, and pay out of pocket to fly him in and out, but the quality time we get is unreal and so worth it. We sometimes will fork out a little extra in flights to keep him with us for as long as we can!

Like everyone else, COVID has made an impact on the way things have panned out. We were stuck in our parent's back yard in our van for nine weeks in April and May 2020. Though not an ideal situation, we made the most of it and decided to renovate our caravan, giving it a new lease of life. It's also held us back visiting some places, as we need Ben to be able to fly freely between wherever we are and Queensland. Obviously, if there are border restrictions in place that restrict movements to Queensland, we avoid this.

While Ben is away, the children and I find somewhere fun to park up, usually a caravan park with a playground and a pool, and we spend our time exploring the area and catching up on chores and school work. I like to park right next to the playground so that the kids can play and I still get a little me time; time to enjoy a morning coffee without the kids all over me, or get some washing done while I can still see them. Playgrounds save my sanity, for sure. And coffee, definitely coffee!

> Survival #3: It's okay not to talk every day, sometimes if you put pressure on speaking on the phone each day, when one or the other is exhausted, it can end in nit-picking or a fight. Sometimes it's good to chat on the phone every second day and just text in between. Communicate your needs with this so that fights aren't starting for no valid reason.

Going from a four-bedroom house on five acres, to a twenty-one-foot living space can only be described as interesting. Though we can have any backyard we want and we've had some fucking awesome backyards in the last year! But when it's raining outside and we have four people jammed inside I would be lying if I didn't say I question if we are crazy for doing this. We have learnt to become conscious consumers, because you just can't take everything along. If it doesn't have at least two uses, it can't come in the van.

Jasmine is in year one this year. We began travelling at the beginning of prep for her. There are many different ways to school on the road, but we have chosen to go through the Home Education Unit (HEU). I create and submit my educational plan for each year, based around her year level's curriculum. While it is based around the curriculum standards, we don't always go about things conventionally. Learning for us isn't about spending hours with her head in a book doing worksheets, the majority of her learning takes place wherever we are at the time!

> **Misconception #1: That the money is great. Yes, it is good. It also comes with a lot of sacrifice, missing events and milestones.**

We do read books and do work sheets of course, but travelling our country has so much to offer. They learn about our primary industries, Indigenous culture, geography, our native animals and so much more. Jasmine is an exceptional reader and we are very proud of how much she has learnt on the road.

One of my biggest concerns was the children missing out on social skills that they acquire from school. Jasmine has always been an anxious little one, who gets nervous around people she isn't comfortable with. I remember a time in kindergarten that she found it hard to say 'good morning' to kids she had been to school with all year!

Within two months on the road, any concerns I had were gone. The thing with travelling is, if you don't get out of your comfort zone and go and speak to people, it makes for a very lonely time! She now can't wait to go and introduce herself and ask if the kids would like to play. Her comfort levels are constantly pushed and she is so much better for it.

As for Finn, he was only eighteen months when we left for our trip. He has learnt to talk, toilet train and interact with others on the road, and he knows no different.

They love nature, animals and most importantly their beautiful country!

I, of course, sometimes get lonely when Ben is at work because I'm usually situated in a town or city where we don't know anyone and have none of our support people nearby. I have always been resilient and capable, but it pushes a whole new level when I'm running solo, knowing my whole family is three states away. Phone calls and FaceTime are a saviour!

Over our time travelling, I have made sure I know the ins and outs of the way the van works, and how to hitch up and tow by myself. This is super important to me. Could you imagine being somewhere for two weeks that you felt uncomfortable? If I'm not happy somewhere, or we are bored, I hook the van up, with my little helpers, and tow it away to explore somewhere else. I do find it easier to stay put for the two weeks, but sometimes I feel adventurous and want to do a bit of travelling solo, and it is awesome to have that option. I always feel proud when we have travelled without Ben, and the look on men's faces when a woman hops out of the big four-wheel drive towing a huge van, is priceless.

We've met some wonderful people on the road, travelling like us, and even some lifelong friends along the way. But if we don't meet any like-minded travelling families where we are staying, sometimes it can be a week without having an adult face-to-face conversation. I homeschool Jasmine, so this keeps us busy, and I prepare the van for our next trip too.

> **Misconception #2: That all FIFO workers cheat on their wives.** I'm not sure about other industries, but in the oil and gas, they are male only crews, though there are females in the industry. Regardless of the crews though, if you can't trust your husband at work there are bigger problems than the industry.

We prefer to free-camp while Ben is with us, meaning we are

self-sufficient and rely on our own water tanks and solar. We get to see some of Australia's most beautiful and remote spots by living this way. I wouldn't say it is cheaper than living in a home, but it is certainly not any more expensive either.

So far we have travelled through five states and territories, with no intention of stopping any time soon. We try to follow the sun, which means we go where the weather is good. The beauty of having a home on wheels is if you don't like somewhere, or the weather is no good, you can easily move on. Likewise, if you really enjoy where you are, you can stick around. We have come to realise that the best plan is to have no plan!

I use our Facebook and Instagram page, 'The Travldeens,' to keep our family and friends up to date and have found it a bit of an outlet, speaking about how we manage our life on the road while also keeping employed with FIFO. Our surname is Fazldeen, so when we began talking to our friends about travelling, it was a bit of a joke that stuck. The travelling community is huge and we get to connect with so many other families who travel full-time as well. There are some that do FIFO too, and it's always cool to meet people doing the same thing as us.

> **Misconception #3: That you are lucky to earn big money. Lucky is always the word used. The men work hard and sacrifice their time with their families, missing out on milestones. Money can't replace these things.**

We often hear how lucky we are to be living this life. There is nothing lucky about our lifestyle, we have had some very traumatic times over the last few years that have helped us realise that life is too short to be sitting around waiting for 'lucky' to happen. We have had to make some serious sacrifices to get us to this point. Ben works and helps support his family just like everybody else, and we have overcome many challenges. I hear people speaking about FIFO workers and how they are blessed to earn a good wage. This is a choice we have made because it suits us, it suits our life, but it is not without sacrifices. You need to be prepared for that and it is not a lifestyle for everyone. Travelling on top of that adds a whole other aspect.

My advice to anybody wanting to travel while doing FIFO is to make sure you are comfortable with the FIFO life first. It can be challenging to get used to being solo and being responsible for the kids alone for weeks on end. You need to learn to be resilient. This is far easier at home where you have a support system. Once you are confident with this, then go for it. You won't regret it. We always say, the worst that can happen is that we sell the caravan and move back in to a house. If all else fails we have seen some really great places and made some fucking awesome memories in the process.

Overall, we bloody love the nomadic life. I am very appreciative of the doors that being a FIFO family have opened for us, and love that it allows us to live life on our terms. We can see ourselves continuing this way for years to come, though we will eventually stop travelling and get the kids into mainstream school. But for now we are right where we need to be and enjoying our time together as a FIFO Travelling Family!

'BEING A FIFO GIRLFRIEND AND LIVING LIFE WITH AND WITHOUT MY FIFO PARTNER HELPED TO ENHANCE OUR COMMUNICATION AND BECOME AWARE OF EACH OTHER'S NEEDS IN A WAY WE HAD NEVER THOUGHT ABOUT BEFORE. I THINK IT TIGHTENS YOU AS A COUPLE, MAKES YOU COMPROMISE AND WORK AROUND EACH OTHER A LOT MORE. IT MADE US LOOK AT THE BIG PICTURE AND NOT SWEAT THE SMALL STUFF SO MUCH.'

Melinda Simpson – 'The Compromising Wife'

THE COMPROMISING WIFE

NAME: MELINDA SIMPSON
INDUSTRY: HARD ROCK MINING - NIPPER (CANNINGTON QLD,
KAMBALDA WA, NYNGAN NSW)
RELATIONSHIP STATUS: AT THE TIME 'PARTNER' (NOW MARRIED)
TIME IN INDUSTRY: 3 YEARS ON AND OFF (2006-08)

It might be a bit too early in our author/reader relationship to be asking this, but I assume you've heard of the 'C' word?

Those of you with a naughty, naughty mind thought of THAT one, didn't you? Don't deny it, I KNOW you did. That, however, my friends, is not the one I'm talking about.

The 'C' words that defined MY journey as a FIFO girlfriend, came as several different ones.

In no particular order of importance, they were:

Compromise

Cuffs

Comments

Community

And ...

A Cat

As kinky as these may sound, these lessons were a sweet and gentle curve into learning to problem-solve and communicate in our relationship. Imparted intermittently by the universe over three years of on/off FIFO, swing changes, late flights, grounded flights, big pay cheques, company changes, interstate swaps, financial crisis, animal rescues and parties of one (nudge nudge, wink wink – how's that hand holding up, big fella? ☺), we did not have the advantage of body language, or facial expressions to take cues from. Misunderstandings, wants and needs had to be sorted out and solved, through breaking comfort zones, goal setting and working through the problem as a team.

#teamsimpsonunited

Although we didn't know it yet, #TeamSimpson, made up of myself and my now-husband Chris, was going to be stronger and more united than ever before.

To set the scene, let's dial back the years – to the noughties. 2006-2008 were part of a decade where Avril Lavigne was still relevant, all fringed ... well everything was flapping off human clothes horses, and despite the financial crisis, mortgage interest rates were 'good' at 7%, or thereabouts. (Yes, I know Karen, back in the '90s you had interest rates of 17%). This was back when Facebook was used to rate girls on their hotness, iPods were peak, and smart phones were a twinkle in Steve's eye. Communication, although on the cusp of exploding, was pretty basic, in a 'noughties' kind of way. Telephones still mostly connected to a wall, the height of coolness, a flip phone had only basic video capabilities. I still read the newspaper - on like, real paper.

#flipphoneswerecool

Yet, like the ruins of Pompeii or the Colosseum, these lessons, memories, and experiences set the path for us to our present day lives. They say that the days are long, but the years are short, and this could not be any truer for us since our FIFO experience. It led to us getting married, having three kids in three separate states, living in three states, and having friends all over Australia.

Just as an aside and before I continue, I should probably mention the 'OMO' myth. I am told that it is true, however I'm somewhat dubious. I have no sources to confirm this tale, but in FIFO circles from the past, it's an urban myth which keeps doing the rounds.

Like any good story let's start at the beginning. We'll get to the cuffs, comments, and cat later, along with the OMO of course!

#theOMOstoryisforlater
#ourjourneybegins #tweakingtheplan #letsalljustgetalong

Our short time in the FIFO bubble was important for us and to us for many reasons, not the least being that we looked at it like our bridge. Getting us from where we were to where we wanted to be.

We had just arrived back from living in the UK; we had empty pockets but bucketloads of memories and experiences. We were still high on travel adrenalin, and with no kids it felt like a game of 'roll the dice and see what life experience comes next.' We had both left home as teenagers, boomeranging backwards and forwards when we felt like it, and as well as being used to living away from friends and family, we were open to what the universe would deliver for the next part of our journey. It just so happened that the universe had decided it wasn't our time to settle into domesticity, and with a phone call coming completely out of the blue one night, Chris received a job offer to start work in a mine on the other side of Australia. He was to begin in five days.

#startthatjobChris

171

I was locked into a permanent job in NSW, so I didn't have the option of moving at the time, but with both of us still restless and seeking the next part of our life adventure, we decided that this opportunity was worth checking out. I had severe travel envy of Chris, sprinkled with a touch of adventure jealousy.

That first time we were apart for four months, and only saw each other for a week during it. It wasn't going to cut it. The possibility of years of this stretched in front of us, seeing each other for a week every five months or so.

Not happy Jan. We had to find a compromise.

We needed to tweak the universe's plan - so we did.

FIFO was the compromise.

#compromiseandsacrifice #FIFObegins
#whatsortofcuffs #nosexytimeshere #moneymoneymoney

For the 99% ers, life is full of compromise, I get it. Everything always looks greener right? Not enough money, not enough family time, too much work, not enough hours in the day and don't even get me started on trying to juggle work and parenthood. Whatever lifestyle we choose requires us to compromise something else. Everyday we make small compromises, swaps and sacrifices to make life the best we can at the time.

The FIFO lifestyle is a compromise for most people. You're giving up time spent with a loved one for maybe some kind of job security, or maybe to earn better money to provide opportunities for yourselves and your families.

What struck me about the mining and FIFO lifestyle the most though, was how egalitarian it was for the time.

An engineer who did a uni degree, could be on the same money as say an Airlegger who dropped out of school in year ten. With many areas in the mining field, you didn't need a uni degree and, in some cases, as with Chris' jobs, you didn't need anything other than on-the-job training. When working in the underground sector, and if you want to you can do your 'shift boss' ticket and go even higher to become an underground manager.

For anyone who doesn't grow up in a mining bubble, this can seem insane, and sometimes hard to wrap your head around. Suddenly, you don't have to scrimp like you used to. You start to think about investments, big houses and the latest four-wheel drive.

#ohwhatafeeling

Baby, at this stage - you got the cuffs on.

Not soft, pink fluffy ones. Not sexy black leather ones. Not even 'madam, you're under arrest for poor taste in clothes' ones.

Nope. You're now held hostage by the strongest ones there are.

You're now held hostage by the 'money cuffs'. #itsarichmansworld

I can't even remember how we came about this saying. I guess somebody said it once, and it stuck. All around us we could see evidence of people we knew in the industry, who had been lured and then bound by the money handcuffs. Bound to credit cards, big loans and becoming slaves to debt.

We too were now hostages. Like a dominant with a choke hold, pay week was a pleasantly tightening noose. When we went back to normal paying jobs years afterwards, it did kind of hurt. The thing with handcuffs, you see, is you need to have the key to unlock them, and you need to keep that key close.

Eyes on the prize guys.

When you've got your prize, you find the key and unlock the handcuffs.

As #TeamSimpson, we knew our prize and we kept our eyes on

173

it. In a nutshell, sacrifice time with each other, for the longer-term goal of having money in the bank and wiggle room with our finances.

We knew this gig wasn't long term for us, and our communication was clear enough that every money touchdown was made to count. Don't get me wrong, it really hurt when those money cuffs came off a few years later, but boy, we had set ourselves a good beginning.

#teamsimpson #makehaywhilethesunshines #eyesontheprize #ifyoucantsayanythingnice #ifihadadollar #shhhhdonttalk #constantsacrifice

Lordy lord.

If I had a dollar for every time someone said, 'Wow, you guys must be on such good money,' or, 'Wow, you guys are set for life,' I'd be retired. *Sigh*

Remember I mentioned words like 'sacrifice' and 'compromise?'

We tried to live this life. We did sacrifice being together. We did compromise and adjust. We also spent a lot of time waiting. Waiting for Chris' off week. Waiting to phone each other. Waiting for a plane to land. Waiting for a taxi to pick up.

While I laid out starfish-style, reading in my bed to all hours of the morning without being asked to turn off the light, #readingheaven, Chris was going to the mess hall and having quality bro time with his new friends. Remember kids, it's not what you know, it's who you know. Although this may not be a completely silver lining, this was very definitely a tarnished copper one.

It'll be no surprise when I say it's bloody lonely when your partner is doing FIFO. We didn't have kids at the time and often while Chris was living it up eating camp food, I was living it up with my bags of microwave popcorn. I ate a lot of popcorn.

Mostly because I couldn't be bothered cooking, because that would then mean washing up, and I mean who really wants to live on spag bol for fourteen nights straight? If you asked me to describe the FIFO years using only a few words, it would look like this.

'Popcorn, sleep, read, work, popcorn, sleep, read, watch TV, work, hang out with friends, popcorn, go to pub, work, popcorn, go to pub, see Chris yay.'

Rinse and repeat x3 years.

My point here is that there will always be sacrifice and compromise to get to your goals. Be like a rhinoceros, have thick skin. Let people talk. People don't know what they don't know.

*#betherhinoceros #letthepeoplejudge
#rescuecat #beprepared #youcanneverhavetoomanybatteries*

One night I got to thinking that I needed somebody to keep me company. Fictional characters just weren't doing the job properly. I needed something more.

Enter, Oliver.

Oliver was a red head who liked to regurgitate his food constantly as a gift to me. He was also a fat red tabby who had been hit by a car and taken to my local RSPCA. He had his jaw wired and was on special food that cost a bloody fortune. Despite these flaws however, he was now my new housemate.

I worked out that the year I got him, Oliver was up to about life number five. The first night I had him he used up life number six. Following the instructions very clearly from the RSPCA (because - 'type A' here, hello!), I locked him in the laundry. Cats, they told me, like to acclimatise themselves to new environments by making themselves at home in small spaces within that new

175

environment. With that firmly in mind, I plonked him and his luxuries in our small laundry.

The only punchline to this story is that about fifteen minutes later I went in to check on him and little Oliver was gone, as in, no where to be found. At. All. He had disappeared in a tiny laundry with only one exit, which I had firmly shut. I checked everywhere. It was a complete mindfuck. I mean where the hell was this bloody cat? It turned out he'd been exploring the laundry and had fallen down the back of the cylindrical hot water system, which was placed in a corner of the room. Like a round peg in a square hole. All I could see was the bum of this jammed-down cat with a flag waving tail showing me how enraged he was.

In normal circumstances I would have said, 'Chris, please come and help me grab the tail of the cat while we pull it out,' followed by a good laugh and a glass of wine. But Chris had just gone back on swing and I was there with just the cat and my popcorn, #crazycatlady.

This is where I was completely unprepared. I needed help. I ended up ringing my close friends who came around and took one look and went, 'Fuck Mel, don't look down here. It's not a great sight.'

Too late on that one people.

My second phone call after much discussion was my new boss. As in, he'd only been my boss for a total of four days. I was lucky that someone had his number, because he was the only person I could think of with long enough arms to pull the bloody cat out.

This was probably the first time I realised I was on my own pretty much most of the time and that I should really put some emergency plans and numbers into place in case, God forbid, something else happened. After spending five years together I had forgotten how to be independent. It was a quick learning curve

I can tell you. With my heart thumping from the near death of my new/old cat, I pulled on my Miss Independent pants and got myself sorted.

#nomuckingaroundhere #preparelikeyoureaboyscout #missindependent

Like the boy scout I never was, I next level prepared for my FIFO alone time.

Channelling Jason Bourne, I equipped myself with details of the following:

- Where the fuse box was and what switch was what

- How I had to change a lightbulb (again)

- How the hell the aerial thingy on the TV worked

- Who my drop-everything-and-run-to-me-person-in-an-emergency was

And the most important of all,

- Making sure I had a never-ending supply of torches and batteries.

Batteries, batteries, batteries of every kind.

Somehow this evolution of thought and organisation led me to the conclusion that I was turning into Miss Havisham; doomed to die with just my cat, wedding dress and a bag of mouldy empty popcorn.

My 'cat getting' epiphany told me I needed to get out and

make the most of this time, to catch up with people I hadn't seen in ages. I had to get out of my comfort zone so I could deal with shit that came up at home in an adult-like manner.

I needed to build a community around me so that when Chris was on swing, I could survive being in adult land by myself again. Such a sweet coming of age story isn't it?

Building a community of friends and family around you IS one of the most important things you can do for yourself if your partner is in the FIFO industry. Communicating and sharing with them what it's like to live a FIFO lifestyle and asking them to be there for you if you ever need that emergency cat rescue like I did, is essential for a FIFO life/wife.

#happylifehappyFIFOwife #findafriend #talkitoutforgoodmentalhealth

Let's all bow our heads to Oliver, who ended up living in three different states of Australia, caught three planes in his little travel box, and ended his life being run over at the age of fourteen. Poor boy.

#Oliverteacheslifelessons

Being a FIFO partner is like giving birth. Until you've lived it, it's hard to realise the emotion attached to the experience. Underneath the gloss of the pay cheque is the real cost of living; excitement, sadness, sometimes depression, loneliness, boredom, relief, highs, hopelessness and love.

It's a veritable rollercoaster of emotion.

Being the completely imperfect human that I am, I'm not in any position to give advice to anyone. However, these are a few of my top tips that might make living a FIFO lifestyle a little easier:

FRIENDS FOR LIFE

1. Don't Become Disconnected
   It's easy to become disconnected from your community and friends. After all, no one wants to be the third wheel at a barbeque. Let your good friends know exactly what it's like and ask them if you can ring them in the case of an emergency or anything else. Join online support groups so you can connect with others going through the same thing.

2. Opportunity Knocks
   Look at this time as an opportunity to level up and spread your wings. What a great time to meet new people and connect with others. Use your time alone (if you don't have kids), to do the things that you've always wanted to do. Challenge yourself by getting out of your comfort zone in some way.

3. Mental Health Rules
   If you're feeling lonely and down (which will be sometimes), talk to someone who is going through the same thing, your partner or your GP. Believe me, keeping it all bottled up just makes you miserable.

4. Make Hay, (and all that jazz)
   Save, save, save. After all, isn't that why you started doing it in the first place? I don't think I've met anyone who doesn't do it for the money. If you don't want to keep that dollar bill handcuff on, find yourself a good accountant or financial planner - or at least read 'The Barefoot Investor' by Scott Pape.

#naughtyhandcuffs #justmakinglifeeasier
#theOMOstory #FIFO #Urbanmyth?

The story goes that when miners were away on shift work, their partners, if they were at home and wanted some ... 'extra action,' would put an OMO box in the front window of the house. The OMO would stand for 'old man out' and be, I suppose, like a 'mating call' to their other partner so to speak. This was not limited to FIFO share houses but to the people living in the mining towns.

Whatever the deal was, I was never game to buy OMO when I moved to a mining town when we finished up FIFO.

#whoknowsifitstrue #DontleaveyourOMOboxinthefrontwindow

'THERE MIGHT BE GOLD AT THE END OF THE FIFO RAINBOW BUT THERE'S PLENTY OF RED DIRT TOO. THAT'S WHY IT'S INCREDIBLY IMPORTANT TO HAVE A STRONG NETWORK OF FAMILY AND FRIENDS; A TRIBE THAT'LL BE THERE TO WASH EVEN THE THICKEST COATING OF DIRT FROM YOUR SHOES.'

Lily Yeang – 'The Resilient Wife'

THE RESILIENT WIFE

NAME: LILY YEANG
INDUSTRY: MINING
RELATIONSHIP STATUS: 8 YEARS DE FACTO & STILL WAITING
FOR A RING
TIME IN INDUSTRY: 4 YEARS

F IFO life is full of ups and downs, and while the money, independence and extra one-on-one time with my partner are great, it's the challenges – and one in particular – we've experienced that remind us that the FIFO lifestyle isn't always sunshine and rainbows (there's plenty of red dirt, too).

My partner entered the FIFO world as a driller's offsider a few years ago. We adapted to the lifestyle reasonably well. There were plenty of positives;

- more career opportunities (for him and for me; I was able to start my own business thanks to the next point)

- more money to set ourselves up financially, and

- more time to spend with each other.

But where there are positives, there are negatives. The money was great, but my partner worked bloody hard for every cent. He was home for longer chunks of time, but missed out on seeing family and friends who had regular, nine-to-five, Monday to Friday jobs. And while we both enjoyed our independence, we quickly realised how lonely and isolating FIFO life can be.

Us FIFO wives and partners have either learnt to be, or are already, quite independent, but there are some things we all agree, are best not to have to go through alone. We were at our favourite beach when I told my partner we were expecting our first child. I had concocted a number of ways to announce the news to him, even before I knew I was pregnant. I could fill our house with helium balloons, hide the positive pregnancy test inside one and make him pop all of the balloons until he found it. Maybe I could wait for him at the airport, and when he came out I could hold up a 'FUTURE DAD' sign, or maybe I could convince one of his favourite football players to send him a video congratulating him on being a first time father.

> **Survival #1: Build a strong support network of family and/or friends that you can rely on no matter what.**

My elaborate plans all fell by the wayside though when an off-the-cuff pregnancy test I took two days into my partner's off-swing, returned a positive result. A little improvisation was now required, leading me to what I like to call 'Plan B.' It was a perfect day for a dip in the sea, so we headed to the coast. We went to our usual spot, unpacked the car and set up shop. While my partner was getting comfy, I retrieved a small pouch from my bag. 'I've got a present for you,' I said, and handed him the poorly-wrapped gift. I eagerly watched him open it. First he discovered the pregnancy test; a random plastic stick that he waved about in one hand, a look of confusion slapped across his face. Then he pulled a babysuit out of the pouch featuring the logo of his favourite football team. Like a light bulb, his face lit up. He has had few speechless moments, and this happened to be one of them. Luckily, words weren't needed to express how happy he was – the tears and ridiculous smile on his face would do.

Fast forward a few weeks. My partner had just flown across the country for his swing, when I noticed I had slight spotting and a dull lower back ache. I had an inkling – a niggling feeling – that something was up for a while, but it wasn't until the bleeding that I really began to worry. Because it was my first pregnancy, I didn't have a clue of what were 'normal symptoms' and what weren't. I remember talking to my partner about it; I didn't know what to do and neither did he. In the end, after umming and ahing, I decided to bite the bullet and call my doctor, who asked me to come in.

> **Survival #2: Communicate well and communicate often. My partner and I talk almost every night (it's not for everyone but it works for us).**

At the doctor's surgery my GP tried to stay positive. 'You might just be one of the lucky few who bleed,' she said, but suggested I go and have an ultrasound just in case. My first pregnancy scan went differently to how I had envisioned it. For one, I had hoped my partner would be there with me. Instead, I found myself alone, lying on a bed in a solemn-looking room with no windows. It wasn't at all how I had envisioned it to be. The sonographer came in, smothered my stomach in gel and began the ultrasound. During the scan he asked how far along I thought I was. 'The gestational sac doesn't match your estimated dates, perhaps you're not as far along as you thought?' he said. I tried to remain optimistic and went home to rest.

I woke early the next morning with intense stomach cramps. It was around 4 am, about the time my partner was getting ready to start work. I instantly knew something was wrong and was hit with an overwhelming feeling of anxiety. I went to the toilet and looked down to find way more blood than before. 'What do I do?' I was pretty sure I was having a miscarriage, but I wasn't losing enough blood to warrant a trip to the hospital. Because we decided to keep the pregnancy between us until the twelve-week mark, no one else knew. I could have called a girlfriend who lived down the road, but she was about to start a new job and I didn't want to burden her. 'Should I call mum?' Deep down I really wanted her around, but she lived two-and-a-half hours away. I didn't want to worry my partner, but this was something I had to tell him. I decided to start there and sent him a text.

I think I've lost the baby.

It's hard to describe the incredible joy we both felt when we found out we were expecting our first child, but it's even harder to explain the feeling when that joy is taken away. My phone rang. I was trying my best to be strong, but I burst into tears the moment I heard his voice. I could barely get a word out; I was a blubbering mess. Although I tried convincing myself I was alright, this was one thing I really didn't want to go through on my own. After a while I managed to mumble, 'You don't have to come home … I'm fine, I'm okay.' But really, I wasn't. And neither was he. He was on the other side of Australia, listening to me weeping over the phone. He couldn't hug me or kiss me. All he could do was talk and listen, and even then, he was due to start his shift in less than ten minutes. It was a shit situation for both of us.

> Survival #3: It's easy to focus on the money, the work and the chores, but always make time to have a little fun.

I sat in bed, numb. A wave of emotions washed over me; a combination of intense sadness, fear, worry and confusion. When you've planned something as important as starting a family, and that gets taken away from you, it sucks. I felt defeated, and there was nothing I could do. Lucky for me, my partner could, and did, do something. He called me back and said he had called my parents, who were already on their way, and that he was in a taxi to the airport. He later told me he was so upset, his supervisor took one look at him and instantly began organising emergency flights home. It would take him almost twenty hours to make it back, but he was coming as fast as he could. Needless to say, I was relieved.

Misconception #1: FIFO workers have heaps of money. You make the money because you work incredibly long hours without breaks or weekends.

Then mum called. I knew she had a lot of questions, especially seeing as she didn't even know I was pregnant, but she reassured me everything was going to be okay and that they weren't far away. They've always been there for me, no matter what, and distance wasn't going to stop them now. I curled up into a ball on my bed and shoved my head in my pillow. I thought I had exhausted my tear quota by the time they arrived, but when dad hugged me the tears came flooding back. I sobbed into his shoulder and then into mum's. Not my finest moment, but I was glad my parents were there to support me through it. We spent the morning snuggled on the couch, watching Rage. ABC was playing a Nirvana special. It's funny what details you remember about a shitty situation.

Throughout the morning my cramps increased in intensity. One in particular, had me rushing to the toilet. As I sat down, I felt my uterus contracting. Yup, there was no doubt about it, the baby was gone. I knew that my body was only doing what it needed to do to ensure a healthy mum and future healthy bubs. I knew that it was getting rid of something that wasn't viable and that it would all be for the best. What I didn't know was how much it would hurt. Physically, I was okay. My body did its thing and before long my cramps were back down to a dull ache. Emotionally? Well, let's just say I needed a bit longer to recover.

I'm not a particularly emotional person; I'm more the put-on-a-brave-face-and-cry-behind-closed-doors type. I also consider myself quite logical, so I understood that having a miscarriage wasn't the end of the world. I was going to be okay. My life wasn't threatened. I'd bounce back. But it still felt horrible. I don't think I've cried so much in my life.

After two taxi rides, plenty of time waiting at the airport, a five-hour flight, then a three-hour drive home, my partner finally made it through the door around 9 pm. By then my cramping had stopped, the bleeding had slowed and I'd had quite some time to process the events of the day - but there were still plenty of tears. He came and gave me a big bear hug and I buried my face into his chest. We were both exhausted but glad we were in each other's arms.

Misconception #2: You get plenty of time off. You do, but you're away from home a lot too, which means you miss things.

Our story isn't unique – in Australia, up to one in four pregnancies end in miscarriage, with the rate of loss significantly higher during the first twelve weeks of conception. In fact, some of the women in this book have also experienced miscarriage. I count myself lucky for not having a miscarriage later down the track, but that doesn't mean my early loss didn't affect me. It doesn't mean anyone who suffers a miscarriage, no matter how far along they are, won't be affected. After it happened, I gained an incredible amount of empathy for women who have been in similar situations. I understood how it felt when good-intentioned people said, 'At least you can try again.' And that sometimes you don't want to talk about your experience until you're ready.

On that note, I made sure I didn't shy away from sharing what happened with close family and friends. It was important to me that people knew, allowing for open conversation around miscarriages, conception and birth, and so that others knew they weren't alone. It's not an easy topic to talk about, but it's one I believe shouldn't be taboo. I thought if I had this experience, surely others had too. Turns out I was right. My mum has had two miscarriages, my sister-in-law one. I discovered a number of friends also had problems getting pregnant and/or had traumatic births.

> Misconception #3: It's a young man's game. That's just simply not true. My partner was in his early thirties when he entered the industry and a lot of his colleagues are around his age. Oh, and there are plenty of women working in FIFO, too.

This wasn't the only challenge my partner and I faced that year. We first got a taste of the harsh realities of the twenty-first century's long-distance relationship when one of my family members passed away unexpectedly. It was the first time I had lost someone so close. Another early morning text was sent to my partner telling him the bad news. We already knew being FIFO meant we'd miss things, but it didn't sink in until we realised we couldn't make it to the funeral. At least my partner was able to come home early. Then, three more family members ended up in hospital for different reasons.

Those experiences led us to learn a lot about ourselves and each other. I learnt how strong I am, and how resilient I can be; how to get over things and when to take time to grieve. He learnt he's more emotional than he thought and that everyone in the FIFO industry is human. That in an emergency, the longest it would take to get home was a day. We learnt how much we loved each other, just how much we wanted a child, and how isolating, lonely and incredibly inconvenient FIFO life can be. On the flipside, we discovered how important a strong network of family and friends can be and connected with a FIFO community who understood the difficulties of working away.

A few months later COVID hit, and things were looking a bit grim. It was a rough year, and we needed a win. Lucky for us, we had something to look forward to; I found out I was pregnant again. When you've had a miscarriage, any pregnancy is celebrated with a massive side of caution. So while we were overjoyed, we were also taking every precaution. Trying to book appointments around your partner's schedule, (especially when he's only got less than a week at home) is a slight logistical nightmare, but he was able to make it to our very first ultrasound. We got to see our teeny-tiny baby growing in my womb and listen to his heartbeat. This time, it went exactly as I had hoped.

The pregnancy was not without a few dramas. I found out early on that bub was on the smaller side of normal, and my placenta might not have been getting as much nutrients as it was supposed to. I ended up with gestational diabetes, and was showing signs of pre-eclampsia. Because I was classified as a high-risk pregnancy, I had to transfer hospitals, which meant travelling an hour each way just to get to the hospital for my appointments. And of course, each of those appointments were scheduled on days my partner was away. I was a bit bitter about it, but knew that plenty of other people had to do the same. The one thing I definitely didn't want to happen, was for my partner to be away when I went into labour. I survived a miscarriage on my own, but I didn't want him to miss the birth of his child.

Thankfully, his FIFO family were unexpectedly understanding, and ensured he was close by, so when the time came for me to go to hospital, he was right by my side. The miscarriage had a much bigger impact on our lives than we anticipated, but it taught us many things, including resilience and patience. Both traits served me well throughout my pregnancy and labour, and helped me to give birth to a beautiful, healthy and very happy baby boy.

'THE SECRET TO HAPPINESS IS GRATITUDE.
GRATITUDE FOR WHAT IS AND WHAT YOU HAVE.
THERE'S ONLY ONE YOU, SO LISTEN TO YOURSELF
AND YOUR NEEDS; BOTH MENTALLY
AND PHYSICALLY.'

Jessica Louise – 'The Holding Us Down Wife'

THE HOLDING
US DOWN WIFE

NAME: JESSICA LOUISE
INDUSTRY: HEALTH SERVICES IN MINING
(ON-SITE PHYSIOTHERAPIST)
RELATIONSHIP STATUS: DE FACTO
TIME IN INDUSTRY: 3 YEARS

'Hi, I'm Jess, the site physiotherapist,' is the introduction I give to people whilst I'm on-site in my role. My story has some extenuating circumstances, (no, not COVID-19) that led me to the decision of becoming a FIFO physio. Have you ever been to the physio and felt so relaxed and comfortable you feel like you can tell them anything and everything? Dive into my journey on what I've learnt, from both the men and women in mining, from their deepest internal pains, to what motivates them to continue working away from their families and friends.

Three years have passed and I look back on how I got where I am today. A physio by trade, I've worked in hospitals in WA, a Sydney private practice and even as a private physio for people who've suffered a brain injury or stroke, teaching them to feed themselves again or walk for the first time since leaving hospital, sometimes six months prior.

It takes me back to a time where my partner in life fell into a deep depression. For almost a year, I kept us afloat both financially and emotionally. I remember trying to figure out how to keep our relationship going, without continuing to enable the situation. I knew I was enabling; taking on all the finances, cooking meals, cleaning the house and putting stress on myself. Out of the blue, a physio friend posted on Facebook that the business she worked for was looking for a FIFO physio. In that moment I thought, fuck it, what have I got to lose? I knew it would help financially, and at the same time I wouldn't be enabling, as my partner would have to fend for himself while I was away, but I would be home every weekend on a 4:3 roster (Monday to Thursday).

Survival #1: Find your 'you' time both on-site and at home – whether it's yoga, walks, or meditation.

I hadn't realised at the time but it was one of the best decisions I've ever made. Not just for him, but for me. It gave me time to be away and do my own thing. It gave me increased financial security. The distance and time away allowed us to find the spark and the excitement in our relationship again.

Being an on-site physio wasn't what I was expecting it to be. In my mind I thought it would be similar to a private practice setting, where I would be treating big, old miners all day long. The company I work for gave us six months of training to be more than just physios. We learnt to assess the ergonomic set up of workstations and cab seats in the HME (Heavy Mobile Equipment), head out with the crews and look at the potential risk of injury they would have, and work with the team, engineers and safety team to reduce the risk of people hurting themselves in the first place; testing the vibration in the various equipment and tooling and running tests to compare and recommend the seats and tools that had the lowest risk of an injury. I've learnt a tonne as an occupational physiotherapist, but also as a female doing FIFO.

> **Survival #2: Eating healthy doesn't only affect your body weight and systems, it can also provide a balance of chemicals in your brain for a healthy mind.**

It hasn't all been easy however, on one of my very first swings on-site, my room was placed at the back of the camp where large groups of guys would congregate outside their rooms and have more than a couple of drinks together. One night I went to put my washing on the clothes horse, and I was sure to place my socks and underwear in the centre so that my trousers and shirts would be surrounding them. I knew I was only going to be fifteen minutes to dinner and back so I didn't think too much of it. When I returned, all my underwear was missing. My first thought was, 'How inconvenient!' as I only had one other pair left (not including the ones I was already wearing), then it dawned on me that someone out there had taken my underwear. The next day, I told some of the workers in my office, and to my surprise, the men in the group kicked up more of a fuss than the women. For us women, you learn to grow thick skin; whether it's people looking and turning their heads as you walk past in the mess, or the occasional inappropriate remark - which I've learnt to shut down real quick by pretending I don't know what they mean, and having them explain the inappropriate remark to me in front of their mates! By the next day, the guys had my room moved to the front of the camp, under the lights and very close to the admin and dining room. There I learnt that most of the men on-site weren't inappropriate pigs, and most of them did care about my safety. They didn't tolerate what was going on, and us women shouldn't tolerate it either.

Eighteen months into the FIFO life, I started to get anxious every Sunday afternoon prior to flying up to site. Flying twice a week was taking a toll on my body and it took me months to let my manager know. I had played it down as if I was wanting a change, but it didn't phase me too much. Within weeks, I had what I now realise was an anxiety attack. I called my manager and told him he needed to get me another position ASAP. I was in tears and couldn't bear the thought of doing any more swings on-site. Within two weeks I was given a role back in Perth and my anxiety settled. In hindsight, I wish I felt more comfortable reaching out with the EAP (Employee Assistance Program) and had spoken to a professional about how I was feeling. I wasn't quite done with FIFO, as I'm now back in the industry, but just needed to process my thoughts, feelings and anxiety. Six months passed and my employers offered me a team leader position that involved touching base with my own team and completing coverage work. I loved my first swing back on-site and hadn't realised I had missed it. This time around I'm doing things differently, making time for myself by going for walks, doing yoga in my room, journaling and reading books.

Survival #3: Create close friends you can trust on-site that you can vent to - because you'll need to sometimes!

Part of the journaling was a book a close friend gave me; one where you write down five things you are grateful for and an affirmation for the day. I've stopped writing in the book now, but I do keep up with the gratitude thoughts when I'm driving to and from work. There are so many things to be grateful for; the increase in pay compared to working in Perth, the stunning sunsets most nights (and I thought Perth had good sunsets!), not having to think about what I'll cook for dinner, and then the opposite for when I'm in Perth and I have all the time in the day to plan and prep for dinner.

I guess I'm lucky my partner has never been the jealous type or had any trust issues. He was also in the mining industry for ten years before we met, and understands the lifestyle and the long days. We speak most nights and our conversations are more in-depth than ever. Giving him his space allowed him to not rely on me, and to find the strength and courage to help himself. FIFO allows us to spend quality time together.

Misconception #1: Everyone spends unnecessary amounts of money on nothingness.

My partner works in the entertainment business, managing and running events and club nights at various bars and night-clubs around Perth. When he started finding his feet again and getting back into the bar and club scene, others asked how I felt about it. To be honest, after all we have gone through together, I just wanted to see him happy, motivated and himself again. I trust him and I trust what we have, whole-heartedly. He knows I absolutely love him, but I don't NEED him. He knows I'm the type that won't stay in a relationship if I've been done wrong, no matter the rollercoaster we have gone through together. Trust and communication allow us to work in the industries we are in.

It's other people outside of our relationship that have concerns; whether it's this beautifully handsome and charismatic man of mine working in bars and clubs to the early hours of the morning, or my safety on-site, being a smaller, (somewhat) young-looking female.

The stereotype of miners being seedy, fat old men, in my experience, is far from the general demographic on-site. The large majority of men on-site are respectful and have an old-school chivalrous mentality, holding doors open for the women and carrying any heavy equipment/objects. For the small percentage that aren't, reminding them they wouldn't want their daughter or nieces spoken to as they had just done, puts them in their place quite quickly. Hopefully they realise their comment was not welcome or called for, and makes them think twice if they try to imply something with the next female that comes along.

Misconception #2: All the men on-site are seedy and rude (don't get me wrong, there are the odd few).

Being a physio, I see a different side to others working on-site; I see people at their most vulnerable. There is something about lying face down, where you don't have eye contact, and the physical touch during treatment, that allows many people to feel safe enough to open up. The combination of being a female and a physio has provided me with a heightened awareness, where I can tell when someone needs to talk or get something off their chest. I hear stories, time and time again, of men starting FIFO to give their family the financial benefits of living a life greater than they did growing up. Allowing their children to go to private schools to have the best chance possible of achieving their wishes and dreams. With this comes a lot of sacrifice though. What they can't tell their families, is that sometimes they feel like a stranger in their own home. They go home to their partners and children who make them feel guilty for being away, but forget they only started FIFO for the benefit of their loved ones. They say they feel they're just a bank service for their children; children they don't really know. They feel guilty for being away, and then hurt when the kids grow up to believe their dad didn't want to be at home with them. The truth is, their families are on their mind the whole time; the families are their 'why,' the reason they are up there, their reason to be safe on-site, and to go home to in one piece. They don't want to stop FIFO, because everyone's livelihood will change. The kids won't be able to do the extra-curricular activities they are used to, and their partners and wives will have to return to the workforce just to keep the mortgage and lifestyle afloat.

A hope I have for the future is that women in leadership roles won't need to put up a hard barrier to be taken seriously, and they can be who they are at work, and be respected. That men will see the value in women being promoted, as we bring a different perspective, understanding and set of skills to the table. This will continue to push mining in the right direction. I hope the culture continues to change, so the small percentage of sexist and inappropriate men will see their actions are not funny and re-think their attitude before speaking.

Misconception #3: You don't want to spend time with your significant other.

For the women out there thinking of joining the Women in Mining community - I say do it! You won't know until you try. There are many benefits financially and to your lifestyle.

'THE BIGGEST STRUGGLE, FOR ME, WAS BALANCE. I LOST MYSELF, MY IDENTITY, DURING THE EARLY YEARS OF THE FIFO JOURNEY. I NEEDED TO ASSERT MY INDEPENDENCE AND FIND MY HAPPINESS OUTSIDE OF MY ROLES AT HOME.'

Michelle Taylor – 'The Distant Wife'

THE DISTANT WIFE

NAME: MICHELLE TAYLOR
INDUSTRY: VARIOUS
RELATIONSHIP STATUS: MARRIED (BUT SINGLE)
TIME IN INDUSTRY: 7+ YEARS

'I don't know how you do it!'
'I couldn't do what you manage and still keep my shit together!'

'Michelle … She's some sort of superwoman!'

My favourite …

'If Michelle can do it … why can't the others get it done?'

I am Michelle and my roles include (but are not limited to, lol); mother, wife, daughter, sister, aunty, artist, small business owner, chef, house keeper, conflict resolution and morale officer, teacher and occupational therapist. Now that I write it down, yeah – it is a lot.

Firstly, I am mum to three amazing children between seven and two years of age, all of which were conceived and born into the FIFO lifestyle. Secondly, I am married but live alone. You see, my husband is a FIFO worker. We have been in the FIFO industry for over ten years, on and off.

I am an ambitious woman. I am driven. I don't doubt my

abilities and never let such thoughts in. I am strong, I am independent and I am determined.

Hubby has worked in many places across Australia and even overseas for a while. We have been through a lot in our time. We have grown together, fallen apart together and ultimately overcome the odds, together.

Ours is a story of a teacher and mechanical fitter, and struggles with mental health and addiction. We had our children in 2015, 2017 and 2019 and live in south-east Queensland, in a quiet semi-rural suburb on six acres.

My aim with sharing my story is to empower wives, partners, mums, and daughters to believe in themselves and chase their dreams.

> **Survival #1: It's cliché but – communication. It is key. We try to discuss what shifts he will be on and consider the time difference to work out a timeframe that suits both him and our home routine.**

This part of our story started in 2017; I was on maternity leave following the arrival of my second baby. We were in the process of rebuilding our home after I burnt it down. (Yep, long story short, the day I found out I was pregnant again I had a cooking incident that saw my sixteen-month-old and myself fleeing the house with nothing but the clothes on our backs!) A friend and her partner came over to visit and she was an occupational therapist working with young children. She shared some stories of the work she was doing and I also shared some of the struggles I had as a teacher. She told me how beneficial OT could be for some of my students. It got me thinking and honestly made me jealous. I had already met my career aspirations. I didn't want to work off-class but I did want to make more of a difference.

So I asked my friend how I could become an OT. Initially, it was a joke. I was a rubbish university student the first time around and almost didn't finish the degree. I swore that I would never return, but I couldn't shake the thought.

Survival #2: Be confident in yourself – you can do it.

After speaking with hubby, I applied for university for a second time. This time I was a twenty-seven-year-old mum of two. When bub was only eight months old I was back at university completing some pre-requisite classes and just after his first birthday, I started the two-year masters program. Hubby was supportive of my choice even though it meant I would not be returning to full time employment during that time.

Just as I started the masters program, hubby was offered a new FIFO opportunity; this one was international. At this stage of our life I didn't care where he worked, as long as he was away from me and the bills were being paid. Our relationship has always been rocky and this was one of those times. He went to work in Nauru as part of the crushing crew. The roster was a 3:1 with good remuneration. The gig certainly made the time away from home worthwhile.

The distance worked well for us. I gained a new sense of identity in my study. I loved what I was learning and finally felt it was the right fit for me. I was on campus four days a week and still worked one day a week. The kids were in day care five days a week and we had well-established routines to cope with our busy lives. I was happier. When hubby came home we were slowly getting back on track. However, when he was home, his days were no longer structured and he would drink from almost the moment he got up to the moment he passed out on the couch.

At the end of my first semester things were going well and

we decided to try for another baby. He was hesitant. He didn't want to miss the pregnancy or our child growing up. For us, falling pregnant was, thankfully, not difficult. At the end of my first semester at university, I was pregnant with our third child. Yep, I'm that crazy lady that already has two under the age of four and is a masters student.

I was so happy. I have always loved being pregnant and now we were going to give our son a younger sibling. I knew this pregnancy would be tougher on my body as I had a lot more on my plate. I was about to turn thirty and I will never forget my thirtieth birthday.

Survival #3: It's not all about the money.

Hubby was away on my birthday that year and was sober. There was no alcohol available on the island due to a Pan Pacific conference being held. He was doing very well. Just before midnight on the eve of my birthday I received a phone call that no FIFO wife wants to receive. 'There's been an accident … The police are here … Gotta go … Call you soon.' I received another phone call around 1:30 am informing me that he was being taken to the station to make a formal statement. I didn't hear from him again until later that evening.

I had some amazing friends who organised a babysitter and took me out for dinner for my birthday. It wasn't until I got home that I was able to speak with him and hear what happened. It turned out he had organised to go to work in the late evening/early hours in the morning (when it was cooler), to put more product through the crusher. On his way to work, along the under-developed roads, a pack of dogs ran in front of the vehicle and he swerved to avoid injuring them. This resulted in him losing control and the vehicle rolled down a hill. He kept his tools inside the vehicle to keep them safe, though this meant they were not restrained. Hubby was hit on the head by his toolbox, and by his report, he likely lost consciousness for some period of time. He was alone, so had no one to corroborate his version of events. When he didn't show up to site, his workmate came to look for him. Though by this time the police had somehow been notified and were on their way. His workmate found him first and sent him back to the house, which was not too far away and the police found him there. Now this is where the whole situation was turned on its head. Those who are familiar with the presentation of a concussion know that slurred speech, delayed processing and a drowsy appearance are common. We still have no idea if he suffered a concussion, though it is incredibly likely. At this stage the police took him down to the police station to 'record an official statement.' Though that is exactly what didn't happen. He was thrown into a cell after having his personal items removed, told he was drunk and they would speak to him when he sobered up. He was not provided with his medication, water or food throughout this incident.

Misconception #1: It's a good thing he earns good money.

This was one of the most heart breaking incidents we have ever gone through and it's times like these when distance is the most challenging. He needed my help and I couldn't give it to him.

When he arrived back in Australia, almost two weeks after the incident, he sought medical attention. He had some residual neurological symptoms and the doctor organised CT's, MRI's and X-rays. Given the delay, it is likely that any injuries had healed or were no longer remarkable as all scans came back with no obvious injuries. Our doctor suspects he was still suffering from Post-Concussion Syndrome.

After this, hubby managed to find some work locally, meaning he was home more for the kids and was able to come to obstetrician appointments with me. I was in my third semester of university, half-way through the course, though with a baby on the way, I needed to make some adjustments to my course program. Fortunately, I only had to extend my course by one semester and was able to take bub with me to class.

We welcomed our third child, a daughter, in April of 2019. She was, and still is, the sweetest blessing we have ever been given. With our eldest in kindergarten and our son recently turning two, I was travelling an hour each way to university three days a week; life was busy, to say the least.

For most of 2019, hubby worked locally so I self-revoked my FIFO wife status. It was the first time he was home to see one of his babies grow up and he seemed to love it.

When 2020 rolled around, it was set to be the best one yet for our family. I was ready to graduate from post-graduate study, our youngest was to turn one, and I would once again, enter the workforce following a long break. Well that all turned to shit pretty quickly!

Misconception #2: That's a great roster for a family.

By February 2020, local work was becoming scarce. Hubby began to get worried, so he investigated FIFO work again. After reconnecting with a mate from high school, he accepted a casual position with a Perth-based company, providing backfill for the bigger mining companies across WA. As the World Health Organisation declared the pandemic he had secured ongoing work. This helped us breathe a little easier.

On March 13th, hubby flew out for work. We had prepared ourselves for a six-week swing as he had to complete inductions prior to starting on-site. Just two days after he left, borders slammed shut. We didn't see him in person again until September!

Hubby's swings were very irregular. He was offered backfill roles to fill staff shortages. Some swings were for two weeks, some were shorter, though as he couldn't come home, he rented an Airbnb in Perth for however long he was off. Initially he would spend this time completing other site inductions for his upcoming work. It was costly. Between the rent, food, Ubers and alcohol costs, he was spending more in a month than I was.

Misconception #3: Being a FIFO wife, you don't need to work.

Finances have always been a source of contention for us. I have previous form for poor financial management, though I have learnt to budget strictly through our tougher financial times and tightened the reins as we added more kids to our family. Given my years of study where I was not working as much and therefore not bringing in as much money, I didn't feel it was my place to lead the management of the family budget. I always felt I had to ask to spend money – even if it was for the kids. I went without things for myself for many years because I didn't earn enough to contribute.

We had discussed these additional bills during his time off and I asked him to try and plan a bit better. I requested that he go and get freezer meals rather than Uber Eats, but all I could do was ask, it was up to him to make a change. And he did not. We keep separate bank accounts and pool money for bills and the mortgage, so I don't see how much he earns. This gives him freedom to spend his money how he chooses. And choose he does. That man loves to shop on eBay. There were very few days when I didn't come home to a package and it infuriated me. You might be wondering what it was he was buying; well what wasn't he buying? He mostly bought car parts on eBay for the old Triton ute we have at home - a car that no one was driving, a car that we were going to let the rego lapse on, a car that he wasn't home to work on. Every day that I came home to another delivery, I wanted to throw it out, burn it or leave it out front for someone to take.

This online shopping hurt me more than I care to admit, for other reasons. You see, hubby has never made much of a deal about my birthday, our anniversary or Christmas. While I don't ever expect expensive or extravagant gifts, I wanted someone to research the perfect gift, something that required thought and consideration. I wanted him to put some effort into me. I wanted my kids to see that mum deserves the extra effort.

On Mother's Day 2020, hubby was still away. Many places were in lockdown and shopping was difficult. In order to show the kids that it's important to show mum appreciation, I asked my daughter's kindy teacher to take her to the shops one afternoon. Yep, the online shopping aficionado didn't bother to organise a thing, which meant I bought my own Mother's Day gift.

Much of 2020 and hubby working away is a blur. I guess because we lived separate lives. Most mornings, hubby would FaceTime the kids and we managed a quick goodnight at bedtime. The time difference was in my favour, as when we were ready to leave in the morning, hubby would be getting on the bus for work, but when we were ready for bed, he was often still working. This meant the kids didn't really get much of a chance to have conversations with their dad. But life went on. I was busy with my final semester of university, returning to work part-time, and our three growing and active children. Communication quickly deteriorated. I stopped asking him questions. I stopped showing an interest in him and he also stopped taking an interest in me. He stopped asking how I was every morning. He stopped asking how the kids were. We stopped talking. We slowly, without realising it, fell apart. And I liked it.

I had become the mother and the father to our kids. I was good cop and bad cop. I was used to managing it all on my own.

It wasn't easy but I knew that I had only months left before I would graduate. I knew that I just had to keep pushing through for a little while longer and I would be done with university. I would have more time for the kids, increase my earning potential and get some balance back in my life.

As I got closer to finishing my coursework, hubby was oblivious. We weren't talking much; we were just living our lives. I didn't let him in because I didn't want to deal with any drama. It was easier to just go on and get shit done because then the finish line was closer.

In August 2020 I submitted my final assessment for my masters. There was no fanfare; no one to high-five, no one to pour me a drink, no one to hug. It was lonely. I achieved a personal milestone but had no one to celebrate with. I was the first person in my family to complete an undergraduate degree and now the first person to complete postgraduate study and receive a masters. The kids didn't understand how much of a big deal it was and it seemed hubby didn't care.

Borders began to open and hubby made plans to come home for a short amount of time. The craziness settled as university had wrapped up and I was working back in the classroom while I awaited my final results and registration approval.

I knew my birthday in 2020 was going to go unnoticed as it fell on Father's Day. It was also our eldest daughter's first year at school, which meant Father's Day gifts from school. Hubby was due to fly-in on September 5th, and the kids would be able to spend the day with their dad and show their gratitude for everything he had sacrificed and all the things he had missed in the year. But on the Wednesday before he was due to fly home, we arrived home at our usual 6 pm and as we were piling out of the car, hubby walks through the door. The older two kids were beside themselves. They jumped up to give him cuddles. Our youngest though, didn't know who he was. She only knew him via the phone and suddenly the man from the phone was here in person. He was bigger. He was real.

All he wanted was to cuddle his little girl, but she didn't know him. This was a huge struggle for him. It caused him to have a tantrum, storm out, and smoke and drink more. He was suddenly a real life person, who smelt of cigarettes and didn't understand her wants or needs. The increased drinking meant he stayed up later, slept in later and was more reactive and short tempered. It was obvious she was more comfortable with me. She did finally warm up to him, but it took her days to allow him to cuddle her.

He left for Perth to quarantine for two weeks before returning to work and we didn't see him again until two days before Christmas in 2020. And just as he returned to site I started work in my new job and new career path - I was finally working full-time again. I absolutely love my new job, it gives me so much satisfaction. I feel happier at the end of the day and more fulfilled.

After his return home at Christmas, he didn't go back. For now, I am no longer a FIFO wife!

The main message I am trying to portray through this synopsis is that dreams are achievable no matter what support you have in place. For me, the drive to achieve my goals was entirely internal. My world would frequently crumble around me but no one knew. I did my best to fulfill the role of the unwillingly absent parent, and some days my best was not enough. And that's okay! At the end of the day, I am human, mistakes are made and every day is the opportunity to start afresh.

'WE ALL HAVE OUR OWN CHALLENGES AND ACHIEVEMENTS AND HOW WE DEAL WITH THEM IS WHAT DEFINES US. FIFO LIFE IS A WAY OF LIFE THAT REQUIRES US TO ADAPT, CHALLENGE, COPE, SOLDIER ON, SUCCEED AND CELEBRATE JUST LIKE YOU.
BE YOU AND BE GRATEFUL FOR EVERY MOMENT OF EVERY DAY. LIFE HAPPENS FOR YOU TO LEARN AND GROW, SO GROW YOUR LIFE BEAUTIFUL AND APPRECIATE IT.'

Angela Knight – 'The Independant Wife'

THE INDEPENDENT WIFE

NAME: ANGELA KNIGHT
INDUSTRY: BUSINESS OWNER
RELATIONSHIP STATUS: MARRIED
TIME IN INDUSTRY: 9 YEARS

I don't feel different being a FIFO wife. I don't whinge and bitch about being a FIFO wife. I suck it up and get on with my day because I'm pretty sure the person I would complain to has something going on that's way worse. Okay, I occasionally whinge about how everything breaks, goes wrong or fucks up as soon as hubby walks out the door. I feel that being a FIFO wife is like being a single mum part-time and a wife part-time; two different women.

I married into the FIFO life ten years ago. I met my husband Sam while he was on break, at the V8 Car Races seventeen years ago. After a few years of hanging out at the races and secretly liking each other, we eventually hooked up. From there, it took just one visit from Adelaide where I lived, to see him in Perth where he lived, to realise I needed to leave my dream job I recently got in Adelaide, to move to Perth, change my life and see how things went with Sam. I must also mention that we didn't hook up for a while because I was dating someone else. Once I moved to Perth, things moved fast between us and felt right. Now we are married and have an eight-year-old son.

Sam has been a FIFO worker since he was nineteen years old, so I moved into the relationship knowing he 'worked away.' At the beginning of our relationship, it was hard every time he went away. I was lonely and missed him, and even though I had a full-time job and two other FIFO men living in the house, I had moved away from all my family and friends. My coping mechanism was to exercise and stay busy with work. Exercise kept me busy for a couple of hours each day, and the bonus were those happy endorphins that kept sadness away. Exercise is still my hobby, and now my career.

Survival #1: Find friends or groups that have FIFO partners so you can support, understand and swap stories with each other.

Our first few years together I wouldn't go out much, check out Perth or do activities when he was away because I wanted to do them with him. I felt guilty he was missing out and might want to do those things with me. However, over the years, I got to a point where I said, 'Screw this.' I had barely seen Perth and was missing out too, so I spoke with hubby about it. I told him I was going to live while he was away, as I felt I was missing out on life!

Now I feel like two people as a FIFO wife. The single mum that gets shit done my way; and the wife that does things for him, things I think he misses out on, meals he is missing, and activities and outings he will enjoy.

One of the benefits of being a FIFO wife is having time to myself. I eat easy meals, go to bed early, and have the bed to myself. I have time to reflect on my day and mothering; see where I fucked up and how can I do better and meditate. I can do all this without interruptions, questions or distractions. I learn about myself and by doing so I'm happy. I do things my way.

I'm stronger for it. I find it is easier when Sam is away being a mum too. My son and I know each other and have our daily routines. We get to have nice private chats and do mum and son stuff. When Sam is back, obviously it's boy time and our son is excited to have daddy home, but our routine gets out of whack. This changes the mood in the house, bedtime is crazy nuts and there are disagreements. I think it's because men feel they need to protect, provide and be ruler of the house. Wear the pants. I guess when Sam returns home to his castle he wants to feel like the authority in the house (which is hard because I'm stubborn and independent), and wants things done his way. Kids don't work that way; they grow and change every day. I do my best to keep him up to date with our son's needs, but it's fair to say, having dad home does disrupt our routine.

It does get lonely being a FIFO wife. In the evenings when I'm relaxing, when I'm horny, when I want someone to take me out for dinner or a day out, when I want to celebrate or vent, my husband isn't there to talk to. It sucks when he's working underground or the mobile phone signal is out of range.

I love my husband and it would be great to have him home full-time and see him every day and night. As much as that could be hard having him in my face every day, we would set boundaries, and get used to living together. I would kick him out on boys' weekends so I could have my quiet alone time.

> Survival #2: Don't be afraid to knock on your neighbour's door in an emergency, such as to save you from a spider/snake, fix something, change a light bulb or open a jar for you. Everything always happens when hubby leaves for work.

I admit, when hubby comes home, it's different; my great eating and not drinking alcohol goes out the window. It's not his fault, I just become slacker, more relaxed and lazier. When he goes back to work, as mean as this sounds, life goes back to normal for me. I take a deep breath and head into single mum mode. I'm focused on my work, our son, healthy eating, running the house, school runs and activities, friends, self-improvement and pretty much things go my way. I clean everything, and tidy up from the slack week. Then one or two weeks later (rosters change all the time), I clean the house, shave the legs and he comes home. I slip into a different mode of living; FIFO wife, doing family things, eating meals he might want and miss out on, seeing his friends and doing my best to stop being so independent, to make him feel needed and included. I do this because he misses out on so much, like birthdays, and I want him to feel happy and included in family life. Because I don't see him much and because he is the bigger money earner, I feel he deserves to do the things he likes.

> Survival #3: Communicate. When they are away text, email, call, video chat, video message, photos; everything to connect you without them feeling they are missing out. And when they are home, lots of verbal communication. Be honest, share how you feel and share other photos you may not have sent.

My friends always ask, 'How do you do it? Being a mum, working your own business and not breaking down crazy or drunk all the time?' To be honest, I don't know, it's just normal life to me. I look at families/couples that have more than one child, or a husband that works in Perth and wonder how they do it. I like that I get me time and then hubby time. Drinking wine helps too, and walking. I cope because I have to. I call or message my sister, mates or hubby when I need to have a breakdown moment, or my son has a sleep-over so I can have a break (video games help keep him busy if I need a break too). I also prioritise my day (write a to-do list), so I can get through everything and hope not to forget anything. The best way to cope is just chilling back with girlfriends and chatting over a bottle of sparkling wine. And when hubby is home, I get to hand over the school and after-school activity driving to him. So I get a break from that, and finally get to have all the conversations and catchups we have missed.

I have always been supported and encouraged by my husband to do what makes me happy, so I changed careers nine years ago to become a personal trainer. As of six years ago, I run and own a personal training and therapeutic massage business from home. I wanted to work from home so our son can have quality time with me.

> **Misconception #1: From the workers – 'We do it for you so you can have a house and holidays etc'.**
> **Me: You choose to work FIFO and if I want something I will go out and earn it or get it.**

We have had a few periods where hubby has been home for months at a time. While it changed our routine, it was great, we made it work, and our son loved spending more time with dad. Running a business from home gives me the flexibility to pick and choose my hours and still be able to work if my son is home sick. It's easier to fit everything in my day. I prefer to work school hours and at night when my son is sleeping, that way, I can get my paperwork done.

Our son copes okay with FIFO as it's all he knows. He is sad the first day hubby goes back to work but I keep up the routine and give extra mummy love to distract him. And for the two days before hubby returns, I remind him daddy is coming home so he can get excited and look forward to seeing him. Having the technology of video chat is fantastic for them to continue to communicate and online video games keep them both connected. I also like to teach my son what I think is boy stuff, like how to burp on demand, and make fart sounds using your arm. Maybe that's why my husband works away, to get a break from my crazy weirdness.

Sam and I have great trust in each other which definitely makes working away easier, and I'm sure it's the same for him. Infidelity is in the back of our minds but we have to trust each other. Our life is not perfect, just like everyone else, which is probably why I don't think I feel any different as a FIFO wife than how others feel in their marriages. It's all I know. It's all we know. Mostly, arguments we have are about communication. If we get slack while he is away, it can feel like he is a stranger by the time he comes home. It takes two of us, and I'm lazy and complacent too, so we need to try harder instead of blaming other things like the internet etc. Although I know he's on a well-deserved break, we can sometimes argue when he's home because I feel like there's another child in the house. He gets into break mode while my life is still moving along as a mum and business owner. So I'm nagging him to fix this or do that, and help with schoolwork, or the dishes. It's frustrating because I feel my workload and to-do list doubles to include his reminders, chores and washing. It's exhausting with the extra person when you only see them half the time and not in a normal full-time relationship. We may have been married for ten years, but it's really like five when you work out how much time we have spent together.

Misconception #2: That we must be rich/loaded because one of us works FIFO.

If there is an argument that happens at fly-out then I will message or email him, because by that time I have cooled down a bit and am able to better articulate what I mean to say, I can be more loving in my delivery. He responds when he is in phone range or at the end of the day call. I never like to leave us angry when we part, as I don't want him to stress over it during his shift until he is able to talk to me again. Stressing all day is a risk to him and those he works with. That ... and I can't stand leaving things unfinished. I've got to have the last say!

FIFO life doesn't mean we are better off financially, although my husband does like to live the good life, as he did as a single man. Me, I'm a tight ass with money unless it's the money I have earnt myself. Everything we have, we have sacrificed for, saved for and worked for. We don't go out and spend on extravagant holidays every year or have fancy toys, but we do okay. We spend on things we enjoy, like upgrading our house, his man cave, my business, the rare holiday and going out when he is home on break.

What would I change? The super early airport drop-offs and the peak hour pick-ups. Oh, and better internet at his work site so it doesn't keep cutting out when he calls. Of course, I would love it if he worked closer to home, but FIFO works for us.

My advice to FIFO wives is to be creative and keep the spice in your marriage, like sexy pics or messages. Communicate and don't be afraid to vent about your days via phone or email. Be your own person and keep busy; the days fly by when you keep yourself occupied and distracted. When I'm not working or doing the mum thing, I try different hobbies; most of them don't stick, but I try. I've done knitting, dot pictures, Lego, colouring and exercise - yes exercise is my hobby and it's the only one I still do, hubby thinks I'm crazy because of it.

Misconception #3: That I would feel odd drinking alone. Nope. I will happily open a bottle of wine and have a glass by myself.

Would I recommend being a FIFO wife? Only to those women who can handle their own company, are brave enough to live alone half of the time, can trust and be trusted, and are strong and independent. If you are dependent and in need of constant attention, then it's likely not for you. And keep a baseball bat or fry pan under the bed for any midnight scares. I personally keep nunchucks under mine. And as much as it sucks and it's sad on fly-out day, fly-in day is awesome.

Thank you for reading my story. I'm just like you, making my way through life with a smile, doing the best I can.

Funny end note: I notice when he comes home he will always do a routine obligatory walk around the house looking at everything like it's been ages since he last saw it, like it's changed or maybe something has been added or removed. Others have said their partner does this too, lol.

'APPRECIATE THE FIFO LIFESTYLE FOR ALL IT'S
BEAUTIFUL CHAOTIC CRAZINESS. MINDSET IS
EVERYTHING. TREAT OTHERS THE WAY YOU WANT
TO BE TREATED AND IF EVER IN DOUBT, PUT
YOURSELF IN THE OTHER'S SHOES.'

Monique Rangi – 'The Beautiful Yet Chaotic Wife'

THE BEAUTIFUL YET CHAOTIC WIFE

Name: Monique Rangi
Industry: Mining; Processing
Relationship Status: Married, together for 10 years with 4 step kids and our own baby due July 2021
Time in Industry: Husband has been in the industry for over 16 years, I have been in the industry on and off for over 10 years. A total combined 26 years of experience between the two of us.

I started my career in mining in the catering and cleaning sector. When I met the man who was to become my husband in 2010, the fireworks flew. He was the only person who looked me in the eyes when I introduced myself. He made the effort to help by grabbing the bins or mopping the floors of the control room. He was kind and gentle, and we got along like a house on fire, but I was in a relationship at the time, so I never went there and left full of regret that I never got his number. In a weird twist of fate, a year later my best friend got my old job and she gave 'the one that got away' my number. He called the next day to ask me on a date. The rest is history and in 2011 our relationship blossomed. Within the year we were engaged.

> **Survival #1: It's all about mindset.** We can't always control what happens to us, but we can control how we react; what we allow and don't allow in our lives and how we allow our daily situation to affect us, as people and our attitudes towards life. I try to see the best in things and be positive. I have found my tribe who are like my family. They love and accept me just as I am, my family and my FIFO lifestyle. I have quotes up on my mirror on sticky notes to remind me every day to stay positive. They are:
> - I can bounce back well. Setbacks are only temporary.
> - Make a PLAN OF ACTION to solve the problems then FOLLOW THE PLAN.
> - Replace, 'Why is this happening to me?' WITH, 'What is this trying to teach me?' Shift the mindset.
> - I will persevere and NOT give up when things get really difficult.
> - I am committed to making mine and my family's future BRIGHT and HAPPY.

Over the next few years, I worked in a variety of jobs including railway construction, catering/cleaning and underground, until Cody was able to get me a job on the same mine site as him as a green labby (laboratory technician). We did opposite swings on a 2:1 and 8:6 roster. I made a huge effort to not tell anyone I was Cody's fiancé as I did not want to receive any special treatment. I wanted to make a name for myself and prove my worth off my own work ethic. The judgements that men hold around women on-site being 'gold diggers' and 'sluts' was made very clear to me at the time. An electrician confronted me, saying he couldn't believe that after just three months I had somehow, not only managed to sleep with the boss, but also convince him to buy a house. He told me I was a homewrecker, that Cody was happily engaged before I came along and decided to fucking ruin it all. I kindly responded that I was, in fact, the fiancé, and after three years together it seemed like the right next move. The look of shock on his face was quite endearing and I reminded him not to judge others until you know all the facts.

After four years of working six weeks away from each other at a time, we decided to hand in our resignations. The company promptly responded by finally placing us on the same shift. I loved working with my husband. He ran the plant, and I was in the lab. We were the dream team and enjoyed the perks of having each other on-site. We were careful to not flaunt our relationship in front of the crew as we knew others were not so lucky to have their better halves with them. Our crew became family when we were away from our family. They would joke that Cody and I were like the parents. We would always look after our fellas as they worked so hard for us. I would often home-bake food for shutdowns or bring in treats. Sunday on night shift would be barbeque night and everyone on crew would be assigned to bring in a plate or meat to share. We shared our struggles and joys together, offered to solve problems and gave advice in the face of adversity. Hell, we even took a holiday with the crew to Bali to celebrate our one-year wedding anniversary. Even now, after years of not working together, I know those boys have got our back and will be a part of our lives going forward.

> Survival #2: Treat others the way you want to be treated. If you're ever in doubt, put yourself in the other person's shoes. Be a team and look after each other. This was a big one for us. Do things together like cooking dinner or hanging out washing, say if you need a hand or for the other person to look after you with a bath or massage or tackling a problem together. Appreciating that we both make sacrifices, and that one job, (stay-at-home parent vs FIFO) isn't harder; they are both different types of hard and they should be appreciated by the other party for how hard they are.

Four years into my laboratory technician job I realised I no longer found it fulfilling and at twenty-eight decided to return to part-time study of Psychology and Counselling while working away. In my first semester on a 2:1 roster, I thought two units would be a breeze, but it turned out to be particularly hard. I would be up at 3 am every morning to study for a few hours before work, work a twelve-hour shift and then come back to camp and study some more. I even ended up with some crazy supportive co-workers who would let me study at work sometimes to keep up with the workload. If it wasn't for them and my extremely supportive husband making endless cups of tea, I don't think I would have survived my first semester.

Survival #3: There is no shame in seeking therapeutic help; whether that be as a couple, individual or family. It comes from a place of strength to seek help, and therapy builds on that strength. Therapy has a bad name of reflecting weakness or that you're struggling, but we all struggle and, in that sense, you're never alone and it is not weak.

It taught us as a couple to effectively communicate. It's a big one to let each other know what our needs are, instead of arguing to get what we need. Communication within FIFO, being honest and in contact on a daily basis is a need. My need was that on shift change, I wanted him to set aside some time halfway through the swing, for a video call before heading to the pub and having drinks. I needed that time to talk and reconnect, without the pressures of home life.

His need was to hear from me early every morning. It was the best way to start his day. We both worked away for so long, that even if he was at home and didn't need to be up at 4 am, he still would be. A text from me helped his day start 'right.' It's the small things that seem insignificant that matter. I also found that when Cody was home, I just wanted him to take over on rugby training drop-off and helping with dinner. Some swings this was easy, but others it was really hard. I learnt that some breaks could be better than others. I always saw him trying even when he was tired, and I appreciated it because I understood just how hard it was to be away.

After volunteering for the ERT team and being captain for two years, mental health is something I became very passionate about. A series of events sparked this passion in me, including responding to a mental health psychotic break rescue, and a number of suicides in the space of twelve months, that at the time sparked a parliamentary enquiry. After watching so many relationships, families, and people that I loved break down over the years, I could no longer sit by and watch. Having a close friend commit suicide on another site was the tipping point. It's something that is seen every day in the industry but hardly spoken about. FIFO is such a complex and hard lifestyle, it affects not only the workers, but the families too. No job should require a person to get to the point where they feel there is no hope, no way forward, that life is no longer worth living. We sacrifice so much when we are away, our freedom and time with families. It reminds me of a prison; you are told what time to start and finish, have set times for breaks and lose the fundamental things we need as humans, like autonomy and individuality. The company, and its need to hit set targets, becomes a priority over your own basic needs.

> Misconception #1: 'Because you are a woman who works in the industry you must have it so easy, the boys must do all the hard yakka for ya, you lucky thing.' This could not be further from the truth. I used to have to work three times as hard to not only prove my worth as a contractor/worker, but as a woman within the industry. This is often taken advantage of because men know and can pick up on the fact that you never want to give management the opportunity to get rid of you or have something against you if you come across as 'hard work' or 'not working hard enough.'

The thing is that one in five Australians will experience a mental health problem in their lifetime. This drops down to one in every two people within the FIFO population. The predominant view within the industry is that it is the individual's need to take responsibility for their mental health. But the employer also needs to understand, that the conditions under which their employees work, contribute to mental health outcomes and psychological hazards. There is a need for a systematic approach;

not just training leaders but coaching and mentoring to reinforce the training. There needs to be organisational change encouraging a culture that enhances mental health, so it is embedded and sustainable.

Leadership commitment is a big one. Often managers do not realise the impact their daily actions have on the performance of their people. Look after your people and positive performance will follow. Recognition and appreciation for workers' efforts goes such a long way. This is not just about individual prevention but organisational, cultural elevation and engagement. Unfortunately, ownership for our mental health is being put on the person and not the workplace. When you hire a person, you hire the whole person. Employers should aim to bring out the best in the 'whole' person; their well-being, mental health, physical health, career health, financial health. And not just integrated into the employee, but also their family and support network.

Misconception #2: 'You're so lucky to have a whole week off and do nothing.' I found this one pissed me off the most. Most of the time I would come home exhausted and life at home doesn't stop for you. All your appointments and daily items would have to be organised for the week off. Trying to make time to catch up with family friends and the upkeep of relationships and self-care was particularly hard, like a juggling act.

What I found most interesting, was when our company finally did get an organisational psych up on-site, it was to assess how they were looking after employees and dealing with change when the company was changing hands, however, they didn't even interview the workers. They didn't deal with those on the front line slogging it out in the heat and dealing with machines breaking down and equipment faults. And being told there is not enough funding for this, or, 'We are understaffed - just deal with it,' creates more of a negative culture. That is where change needs to happen, on the forefront, interviewing front-line workers to see where the company can improve, not with upper management, but those on the ground dealing with the daily issues.

After five years as a labby, in 2017 I left my job to take over full-time care of my stepson and continue with my studies. I had naïve ideas of what mum life would be like; days at the beach, coffee dates with friends. How very wrong I was. My perfect routine FIFO life got thrown out of the window as I got dunked into the deep end of motherhood with a particularly hard case child. With the hubby on a 2:1 roster, he would come home exhausted struggling to help out.

> **Misconception #3:** 'You must be loaded/make a shit tonne of money.' UMMMMM no not quite. We get taxed a heck of a lot, still have bills and family to support. I still have to work to a budget and ensure all our ducks are in a row; for example, ensuring we have income protection for working in a high-risk industry, a Will is in order, or have savings for unexpected situations.

I was studying full-time, running Kai around to sport six days a week, volunteering at school, working part-time, looking after a sick family member, trying to be a wife, friend and sister and basically had it held together with a glass of wine and a cheese wrapper.

I was dealing with daily abuse from my stepson, both physically and verbally lashing out over simple things like getting up and ready for school. At that time Cody also had two major shoulder reconstructions and somehow, I had become a full-time mum and carer.

In the May 2019 Mother's Day, I had to pull our son out of school for two weeks due to a mental break that I had. I wanted to spend some time at my mum's in the country, and Cody didn't seem to understand why I needed extra support, why somehow this super woman juggling act had fallen apart. I told him two weeks in a kid's life is nothing and Kai wouldn't remember, but he disagreed. I went against his wishes, flew my mum down and we made plans to drive back to the bush the next day. I am not one for ultimatums, but I told him that either I go to my mum's for the help I needed, or I would be gone. Divorce was on the cards and Kai would be his responsibility.

My mum did her best to make Mother's Day amazing by making gifts and a beautiful dinner for us, to which Kai responded by refusing to eat dinner. After I gently asked him to 'please eat your dinner,' he told me to 'fuck off,' that I 'wasn't a real mum.' He said he wished I was dead, that I was a cunt and he wanted me to 'jump off a cliff and die.'

My career, promotion, freedom, everything I had given up to look after him was not appreciated. I reached my breaking point and slapped his face. I wasn't sure if it was the shock or rawness of me telling him that he was never allowed to speak to me like that EVER AGAIN, but he changed that day. After almost two years of compassion, patience and understanding, being kind and calm even when faced with his anger, of understanding it came from a place of hurt and rejection and I was the closest one to take it out on, I was DONE. I could not take anymore. All that I had promised to my husband when we got married, for better or worse, for accepting and loving his children as my own, was really being tested.

I realised that we are in control of our reaction to everything. For a long time, I felt victimised, having to deal with the abuse and tantrums on a daily basis on my own. Then I realised that even though I was reacting calmly and in a consistent manner to Kai, I was allowing it to affect my mental health in big ways. I hid my inability to cope until things came to an absolute head.

I now know I should never have let things get that far. I should have sought help and support from Cody earlier and been honest, before I completely broke and became resentful. The thing is, we can't control how others act towards us but we can control how we react, and how we let people's actions affect us. We can choose to live life being unhappy or we can be proactive and facilitate change by voicing what we accept and won't accept in our lives. Thankfully since then my relationship, both with our son and Cody, has improved, but it took me returning to FIFO work to allow that to happen.

My husband took his long service leave to have his second shoulder op. I told him that as soon as he was capable, I was out, and it would be his turn to be a full-time dad. In August 2019, I did exactly that and got a job FIFO on a 2:2 roster. The boys only lasted ten days.

I came back early to fall in with my normal swing and the night I arrived home, went straight to bed. Cody woke me at 2 am that morning to tell me how sorry he was for not doing more to help when I was the full-time mum. He hadn't realised just how hard it was. He thanked me as he told me how grateful he was for all I had done.

For the first time ever, the boys had to adjust to life without me and with each other. The adjustment period was hard on them but finally I was fully appreciated and valued for what I did. I understand not too many FIFO wives have that luxury, nor do the men really realise or appreciate just how hard it is to be a stay-at-home parent.

Being a stay-at-home parent is fucking hard. Being up at work and away is also hard. It isn't that one is harder than the other - they are both really fucking hard. They are different types of hard. Sometimes it's not until you have been on both sides of the fence that you can really appreciate it. To not be there and kiss your family goodnight after a hard day is heart breaking. Going through emergencies at home without your partner's support to keep your sanity is hard. Emergencies can be even harder when you are thousands of miles away, unable to help in any way other than messages or phone calls, or waiting for the next plane out.

Cody struggled with the fact that he could run a multimillion-dollar plant and a team of five successfully every day for ten years, but couldn't get Kai out the door and all house responsibilities sorted on time on the best of days.

While working away, I struggled with being the super positive one at work and dealing with the negative attitudes on a daily basis; being negatively dragged down took hard work to not let those bad attitudes affect me. I always had my mega boom to play my crazy disco music. Music has become a way of life for me. I was known as the crazy positive disco lady at work. By putting in the effort to uplift and support those around me at work, by the time I got home I struggled to have anything left to give. When you live and breathe FIFO culture for two weeks, it's hard to come home and swap over to family life and keep a positive good attitude. Holding it together for so long at work, when you're home you can finally relax and sometimes that brings out the ugly bits too.

When Cody shared his struggles of being a stay-at-home dad, I felt resentful. He had to look after Kai, the dogs and recover from his operation. By this time Kai was making friends, doing well at school and was a well-adjusted student. To me that was nothing, I thought he had it so much easier than me. Yet I totally misunderstood his struggles, even though I had previously been in a similar situation. Cody struggled with the isolation, and not having the support of the crew and tangible daily outcomes to achieve that he'd had at work for all those years. Any parental achievement and appreciation had to come from me.

The thing is, we may not be in the same boat but we are all in the same storm. Some of us may be in a yacht or a canoe, either way the water is rushing in and some might be drowning. Everyone's experience of a problem is not the same and it's important not to judge based on our experience, and to be kind and help where we can. To be thankful and appreciate the other person for their achievements without comparison. To encourage others to look for their strengths and harness them.

Cody and I have worked FIFO separately and together and we've both been stay-at-home parents while the other is away. We've now decided to take on a new adventure. We are being a 'normal couple' for the first time in ten years in our relationship and now both live and work in Perth; both parenting Kai, and Cody working full-time. Cody made the break into the construction industry, working on machinery which is something he really loves. The exit plan out of FIFO was not easy, but somehow, we've made it. I am finally finishing off my degree with the aim of working within the realm of FIFO mental health and FIFO families long-term. I'm planning to construct a program that caters to FIFO families and helps them to adjust to FIFO life, as well as support them throughout the journey so that everyone has the best chance of success within the industry. I am looking to facilitate real change. Mental health is slowly losing its stigma, but there is a huge amount of work to be done at an organisational and cultural level.

This is the most amount of time Cody and I have ever spent together, and so far, we haven't strangled each other (lol), so we must be doing okay. We are expecting our first child in July 2021 and look forward to undertaking this adventure of parenthood with our pups and Kai.

Our plan is to build up and support families either when they enter or exit the industry as both are huge steps for families to take. Hopefully our experience and passion for the industry will shine as we look to invest in and help others.

My FIFO Mantra: We remember that nights alone aren't permanent. We appreciate that for true love both parties make sacrifices. We also remember, although hard at times, we are lucky to have someone to miss while we are separated from each other, and even more to look forward to when they come home. And that is the 'Beautiful Chaos' of FIFO family life.

'LIFE CAN THROW US CHALLENGES BUT IT'S THE
LESSONS LEARNED THAT GIVE US OUR GREATEST
GROWTH. CHALLENGES ARE HARD, THEY FORCE
US TO MAKE CHANGES AND CHANGE IS HARD. FIND
THE LESSON IN THESE CHALLENGES AND MAKE THE
CHANGES. THE PERSONAL GROWTH LEADS YOU TO
DISCOVER WHO YOU TRULY ARE. I LEARNT THAT I
AM AN INDEPENDENT, RESILIENT WOMAN. I ALSO
LEARNT THAT I'M NOT ALONE.'

Tanya Bolt – 'The Maverick Wife'

THE MAVERICK WIFE

NAME: TANYA BOLT
INDUSTRY: SHOTFIRER
RELATIONSHIP STATUS: INDEPENDENT (HATE THE TERM SINGLE)
TIME IN INDUSTRY: 7 YEARS WITH MY PARTNER, 3 SEPARATED
(NEVER MARRIED)

W here to start. I guess at the beginning.
I met my daughter's dad online. He was on a 2:1 roster when we met, and initially we had a struggle to meet up for our first date due him being at work and when he was home on break, I was off to Sydney for a holiday. We talked, emailed and texted so much and so easily, that the first date was amazing. The first kiss was one of the best I've ever had. It was the heel-kick kind, you know the one when your foot kicks up behind you as a response.

With me working full-time and demanding hours in the city and him juggling his time at home between me and his mates, we very quickly realised it was easier to move in together so we could spend as much time together as possible when he was home. So, after just three months of dating, he moved in with me. Not long after he moved in, I got really sick and doctors put it down to stress. I decided to leave my job to go freelance and this gave us the flexibility to spend even more time together when he was home.

We enjoyed the same things, camping, fishing, the beach, barbeques and the outdoors, so for the most part, in the early days, things were perfect.

> Survival #1: Don't separate your life. It's easy to focus on catching up with their family and friends when they are home as you have the opportunity to catch up with yours while they are away, but keeping your friends separate from them doesn't allow people to see and understand your lifestyle.
> My FIFO partner was shy when he met people and normally, I am the sort of person that can start up a conversation with a chair. I thought it was best to not put him in the position of being uncomfortable, but that was wrong of me to make that decision for him. Over time his comfort with my friends would have come. When I ended our relationship, the common comment I had from my friends was that they couldn't pass judgement on him or our situation because they just didn't know him, even after so many years together.

We did have a few teething issues though as we had both been single for quite some time; there were a few hurdles to get over. If I am honest, we were both selfish with our time. He wanted to fit in the usual time with his mates and I am a self-confessed workaholic but I wanted him to prioritise his time with me. Initially we struggled to work out what time we would spend with each other, but eventually we settled into a routine.

When things were good, they were great. The occasional night sitting up sharing a few red wines after cooking dinner together and just talking were amazing. The connection we had from our communication was almost as intoxicating as the intimacy.

One thing I learnt to embrace about FIFO was that the guys are away long enough for you to miss them. At first, I used to hate him being away and was yearning for him, but then I began to focus on what was good about it. Because I missed him so much, when he was home the intimacy, for me, was always such a powerful connection.

A few years in we had some issues with his gambling. We

had separate finances at the time and it was easy for him to hide how much he was spending. The trust was lost and we did split up. He stayed in the house in another room as I did still love him and wanted to help him and support him while he sorted things out. We talked so much during that time that we eventually got back together and were engaged a year later. I found out I was pregnant a few months after the engagement.

> **Survival #2: Communication.** We had a family tragedy that rocked our family to the core. A child was lost in an horrific accident just three weeks before our daughter was born.
> I've always considered myself to be the one that holds things together in my family and never liked to burden my partner with my 'problems.' He worked twelve to fourteen hour days in ridiculous heat away from his family so I never wanted his time at home to be dealing with my troubles.
> I could have opened up to him and told him that I was hurting, struggling and some days just wanted to lay in bed and cry.
> I had our daughter to care for and a business to run so my emotions got pushed to the side.
> Perhaps if I had opened up to him, things might have turned out differently.

2014 was a year of challenges. Three weeks before our daughter's birth we had a family tragedy where a child was lost in an horrific accident and family members were seriously injured. It rocked my entire family to the core, and we all had issues with how we dealt with it. Myself, I shut down and was always quick with the 'I'm fine' response when anyone asked, especially him.

I will say one thing for the industry and the supervisors, when grieving over our loss and also with the birth of our daughter, his company gave him plenty of time off to be with me to make sure I was okay before he had to go back to work. It was a very difficult time, and I was so grateful that I did not have to go through it alone. I come from a close family so when one of my siblings was grieving the loss of their child, I had mixed emotions, knowing I should be joyful at the upcoming birth of my own child. All I could do was plead with the doctors to wait as long as they could, so there was a distance between the dates. Knowing I wasn't home on my own was comforting.

> **Survival #3: Lose the mask.** I always felt I needed to play 'happy wife' when he was home. My stress, burdens and troubles could wait a week and I could deal with them when he was away again. This does not work. The issues manifest into bigger and bigger issues for yourself and you start to seriously lose who you are. I lacked respect for myself because I knew I wasn't being honest. And how could I ever expect him to respect me if I did not respect myself?

The stresses seemed to add up over a very short period of time. Not long after our daughter's birth we found out the house we were living in was being sold and we needed to move out. We decided to buy a house, though I don't think either of us were very happy with the final purchase. But with a new bub we needed something, so probably rushed the decision, however we made the most of it.

When I reflect over this time, I think we were both screaming on the inside but neither of us wanted to burden the other with our problems. I was a mum with a new bub and a business owner doing it on my own while he was working twelve to fourteen days in forty-degree heat. We were both stressed when he was at work. We should have been supporting each other and releasing our emotions during the six days he was home, but we both tried to deal with it in our own ways.

I learnt early on that he needed 'boys' nights' to let off steam. If this didn't happen then an argument would be guaranteed. It was easier, for the sake of a pleasant rest of the week home, to just roll with it. When things started going downhill, the boys' nights started to turn into two nights. At that time, it felt easier when he wasn't around so I just went with it.

Eighteen months after our daughter was born, he confessed to me that he had been using meth and that his gambling was starting to become an issue again. I honestly thought in the lead-up to the conversation that he was going to tell me he was having an affair as he was staying at his mates at least two nights a week, and money was being taken out of the account in large amounts.

I firmly believe he was depressed during this time. He was away from his new child and I'm sure he missed her like crazy. Coming home to a partner whose only response was 'I'm fine,' and who preferred to work than sit down and discuss what was really eating her up inside, obviously didn't help. I barely slept and I know I was a moody bitch.

> **Misconception #1:** I get paid a lot in child support because my child's dad is FIFO. I hate when people assume this. Just because my daughter's dad is FIFO does not mean I get paid a massive amount in child support, nor does it mean I got a massive settlement. We had our issues, and the split was tumultuous, but I respect what he sacrifices by choosing to work in the mines. He works bloody hard for his money in tough conditions away from his daughter. I have my own business and earn enough to support myself and my daughter, so I chose not to pursue a settlement nor child support when I left. He wanted to care for his daughter as much as he could when he was home, so we go 50/50 in all expenses for her.

We stuck it out for another eighteen months. In that time, I had a miscarriage. Everyone else seemed to brush it off as a common thing that 'all women go through,' so I did too, but it ended up seriously affecting me. Nearly four years on and I still think about the child that would have been a brother or sister to my daughter. I wonder if I had stayed and how things would be now if I had that other child.

I felt like I was on a train wreck waiting to happen but had no idea how to stop it. It was odd as it felt like the impending crash was on pause each time he flew back to work, but would reset again as soon as I picked him up. All the stresses over this time and us not discussing any of it, resulted in him gambling, drinking and using meth. For me, I was drinking, and had severe social anxiety. I was about to lose my business as all my clients were leaving.

I continued to give the 'I'm fine' response whenever he asked if I was okay. I found it easier to be around other people as I was good at putting on the 'happy' mask while screaming inside. I started losing respect for myself and busied myself with trying to make everyone else happy and throw myself into my work. Of course, this was so I didn't need to deal with my issues. I was so focused on hiding how I felt, I failed to see how he was feeling or that he needed my support.

> Misconception #2: I'm an independent (hate the term single) mum half the year and a single woman the other half, what a lifestyle I must have. Sure, I only have one child, it must be so easy for me ... wrong! One kid and no support when he's away. If I get really sick, I have nobody to back me up when it's my week with my daughter, and I struggle through that. I bill forty to sixty hours a week in my business so on the weeks I have my daughter I work less to spend time with her. Then I have to pull extra long days and nights to get back on top of my workload before she is home again. I barely have time for weekends as I'm always working.

The hardest thing I've ever done was to leave him, but I was so lost. Not having him around every day to support me or for me to support him, led us both down a path of depression. We went our separate ways, and both of us went through a lot of personal growth and healing from being apart. We are quite amicable in our relationship now as we co-parent our daughter.

Even though I left, my life is still dictated by the FIFO roster. If you have a child with a FIFO partner, then it is a long-term commitment whether you like it or not. His roster is 8:6 and he has our daughter pretty much the whole six days he's back. When

I take holidays, I work it around the FIFO roster so as not to take time away from his daughter.

I've had my own business for ten years now and have to juggle my work during school hours to get as much done as I can and still spend time with my daughter. I end up working late in the evenings to get things done, but when he is home, I know I have six days to catch up. So I guess my work cycle is on an 8:6 roster too. My daughter is not at an age to be left at home on her own and school time is valuable work time for me, so my exercise routine is on the 8:6 roster also.

Misconception 3: He's on holidays when he's home. No, he's not! He's on an 8:6 roster and picks up our daughter when he flys in and drops her back the night before flying out. He works while away and is a full-time dad when he's home. A six-year-old with no siblings is no walk in the park to keep entertained. Sure, she's in school for some of that time but surely he deserves some downtime after working twelve to fourteen hour days when he's at work.

'I NEVER KNEW HOW HARD IT WOULD BE RAISING CHILDREN SOLO FOR THE MAJORITY OF THE YEAR. I HAVE NEVER FELT SO ISOLATED OR LONELY IN THOSE FIRST YEARS OF BEING A MOTHER. I RESENTED MY HUSBAND LEAVING AND FELT HIS LIFE HADN'T REALLY CHANGED, WHILST MINE WAS TURNED UPSIDE DOWN.'

Taryn Prince – 'The Resentful Wife'

THE RESENTFUL WIFE

NAME: TARYN PRINCE
INDUSTRY: OIL &GAS/MINING
RELATIONSHIP STATUS: MARRIED
TIME IN INDUSTRY: OUR WHOLE RELATIONSHIP 10YRS

I grew up in Karratha, a mining town in the Pilbara, Western Australia. I have been around the culture of mining and FIFO my whole life. Once I hit my late twenties I decided I too wanted to cash in on the mining boom. I was offered a job as a mine site cleaner; a role that paid ridiculously well. It was a no-brainer. I was only a few weeks into this new job and I had already bonded with the other girls who had a tradition at the end of the week, 'Friday night, turn right.' Instead of heading home after work, we'd turn right and go to the Dampier Mermaid 'Home of Red Dog.' It was there that I saw him. He was so manly and rugged in his hi-vis, sleeves rolled up, tattoos showing, red dirt on his face. It was love at first 'site.' We were seeing each other after only a month into my new job. I'd get so excited to be rostered to his area, I'd leave notes in his work bag and treats on his crib table. I always hoped I'd get to see him as we drove through his site area. I will never forget our first kiss. I had climbed under a barbed wire fence to get into his camp one weekend, very classy, it was the best first kiss I'd ever had. I think that's when you know you are on to something, we just wanted each other. We were both on the same roster of five or six weeks on and a week off. Every Sunday was an RDO due to the long roster. As I was residential and his camp was in town and not remote, we could go out to football games, restaurants, pubs, camping. We were cashed up and care-free, drinking and partying, pissing our money away. It honestly was the best time; sneaking into camp, rocking the king single, driving into work together. It wasn't long before he moved out of camp and into my parent's house with me. Six months into our relationship we were engaged and on our one-year anniversary we were married in Eco Beach, Broome. In that first year together we travelled overseas twice, interstate a couple of times, purchased a car, paid off debt, paid for our wedding and relocated to Perth. We were on such a good wicket.

> **Survival #1: Communicate - with each other, constantly, about everything. And to friends and family, don't be afraid to ask for help.**

After our honeymoon, things got hard. Our contract ended in Karratha and I had been working locally in Perth as a travel agent while my husband was FIFOing to inland Pilbara. Both my husband and I struggled being away from each other. My family was still in Karratha and I was newly married with a 4:1 husband. Everything revolved around his work, our wedding was on RNR, our honeymoon on RNR, his thirtieth birthday trip on RNR. We just wanted to be together. We had spent every day together for the first eight months of our relationship and now we were just existing separately - it was time for me to go north again.

This was the first time for me to fly to site, previously I was residential. I was hired as a Peggy (minesite cleaner). It was hard, it was hot, it was daunting; I was stepping into a perceived 'man's' world. I was completely out of my comfort zone, but I knew we had to do this so we could be together. It was the best decision we made. We worked hard, we saved money, we made amazing friends, some of which we are still friendly with now. When you are living there nearly ten months of the year, these people become your family. After six months we upgraded to a double donga, going from a king single to a double bed was heaven!! We had a permanent room, we had a routine, we sat on the bus together and by the end of the contract we even sat in crib together for smoko and lunch. Some couples don't work well being together, but we did, we loved seeing each other every day. He gave me butterflies whenever I would spot him working hard in his hi-vis and hard hat. By the end of the contract I had moved up to 'leading hand Peggy' which meant a pay rise leaving me not too shy of the same income as my husband. Again, we were living life with no responsibilities, at work for the majority of the year and when we were home we would be travelling, eating out and enjoying life. When our contract finished we celebrated by renewing our vows in Las Vegas (yes I've been married twice … to the same man), and managed to put a deposit down for a house in the South West.

> **Survival #2: Have an end goal - whether it's financial, X amount in bank, own home, be debt-free … or when you hit a certain age or your kids hit a certain age. There needs to be light at the end of the tunnel.**

We had a couple of months off between jobs and then I was hired back up to a different site in the Pilbara and my husband got a job on Barrow Island. He wanted Barrow, but for some reason it never appealed to me. I only lasted a couple of months at my new site without him. I felt it was pointless being on two different sites on different rosters, we would never get to see each other. I went back to my travel agency job in the city and he continued doing the 23:10 roster whilst we built our home. Again, I didn't like being away from him. He had to do an extended roster so I took the time to travel solo driving from Fremantle, WA to Darwin, NT. It took me back to my backpacking days. Travel is what I love to do. He met me in NT on RNR and we drove back through the middle together. It was at this point that my biological clock started ticking. I never wanted children, it wasn't in our plan, however one day I woke up and turned to him and said, 'I think we need to have a baby.' We were pregnant a month after returning from our trip. We were living in a share house with my best friend waiting for our home to be ready. My friend also travelled a lot for work. I would be on the floor of the shower every morning vomiting from pregnancy while both my friend and husband were away. I lost 5kg in the first three months. There were days I'd freak out that I would choke on my vomit and no one would know as I was there by myself. Pregnancy irrationalities and hormones are ridiculous.

> Survival #3: Take time to be together when you can; date nights, grocery shopping together when kids are at school, cooking together. You need to remind each other why you are doing this and who you are doing it for. Love each other as much as you can.

FIFO wasn't particularly hard when we worked together, life in general wasn't hard when we were FIFO, everything became hard when we built our home in the South West, with no family or friends and were expecting our first child. Life changed dramatically ... for me. Suddenly I was heavily pregnant with a new puppy (what was I thinking?), and my husband was still on a 4:1 roster. We didn't have any furniture and our TV wasn't hooked into a signal. The first swing in my new home I was sitting on the floor with a giant belly, a puppy curled up in my lap, watching old DVDs between unpacking boxes. This was probably the beginning of where I started to feel isolated; it was the start of what was to come.

We gave birth and our son was four weeks old when my husband went back to work. I was on my own with a four-week-old, and my family, also in mining, were now living in a different state. I had no husband, no friends in our new town, I felt we were on one of the worst rosters. I slowly started to despise him, I resented him. His life hadn't changed, he still got to go to work, he still could chat with his work mates, sleep eight hours a night, go to the wet mess. Our life of travelling, partying, friends, family, and work had disappeared. I was awake constantly. I was breastfeeding constantly. I wasn't eating. I was crying constantly. I didn't bond with my child. I felt so isolated. He would come home and feel like he was 'walking on eggshells.' I just wanted help, I wanted him to 'do everything.' He couldn't, he didn't know how to and if he did do something, I'd criticise him and tell him he was doing it wrong. He couldn't win. Our house and our baby, was, in my mind, my house and my baby. I was the one who was living it 24/7. I had no help, I just had to get on with it. He had no idea what I was going through. We fought a lot. I hated being a mum, I hated being a wife, I hated where we were living and how isolated I was. I wanted to escape. My whole life, whenever anything got too hard, I always just grabbed my keys and went for a drive, or I'd book a flight and go on a holiday. I couldn't do this now. I was stuck. I had to take care of this little human who relied on me for everything. The only thing I feel that kept us together in those first six months of being a parent was the fact that my husband was completely and utterly in love with me. With everything I threw at him, he still wanted to be a family. In hindsight, I feel for my husband. It would have been so hard for him. I see the tears in his eyes every time he kisses our kids goodbye. Now it breaks my heart, initially I was just angry that he would leave us. I never thought that he was devasted to leave us. I never thought he was doing this because he had to, because it was his job. I just resented that he could fly back to site, sleep, and enjoy beers with his mates after work, while I was literally having the life sucked out of me.

When my baby was about eight months old my husband and I started to get back to a good place. Our child was becoming easier to take out and about, and when my husband came home on RNR we started enjoying the breweries and wineries and going to restaurants. We saved money and put it into our house. Every RNR we'd do a new project on the house together; flooring, gardening, concreting. We had a naming ceremony for our son and all my family and his best friends flew over from interstate. We weren't fully back to being who we once were but we were getting there. Then, we fell pregnant again, unexpectantly.

> **Misconception #1: 'We are rolling in the cash,' ... couldn't be further from the truth. As two young single people, yes, with no responsibilities, yes, but once you start a family we went down to one income with two children and a mortgage. Now it's about making ends meet.**

We weren't planning on another child. I struggled initially with our first and our relationship was put to the test. The thought of doing it solo with two under two was scary. I did come around to the idea though and started to become excited; I thought it was meant to be. But everything about this pregnancy felt different. I didn't feel nauseous, I didn't feel right. I became concerned about losing it and they were such strong feelings. Our first scan at ten weeks had a strong heartbeat, however, the fetus was measuring at eight weeks. This didn't add up for me and concerned me. My concerns became a reality when I was told two weeks after my first scan that there was no longer a heartbeat. Of course my husband wasn't home for this, he was due home later that afternoon. I was in the ultrasound with my nine-month-old, in a pram, alone. I spent the next two days bed ridden, had intense period-like pain for a few hours and then there was this miniature baby, two eyes, little legs, arms and teeny-tiny fingers. I have never in my life been as sad as I was in that moment. I never realised what women go through physically and mentally when they lose a child. It is such a horrible and confusing feeling of grieving for someone you have never met. It was then I decided we would definitely have another child to complete our family and within three months we were pregnant again, and later gave birth to another beautiful boy.

> **Misconception #2: 'It's a choice.'** Yes it is, however sometimes it's the only choice. We live in a small town, and my husband's qualifications aren't needed here. He has to travel for work or he wouldn't work.

That first year of having two under two wasn't all love and roses. I struggled. I was solo parenting a newborn and a toddler, I was co-sleeping, and I was isolated. 'It takes a village to raise a child.' Really? Where was my village? It came to a head one week, I was done. I had never felt so much anger and it was starting to concern my parents. I was on the phone to my dad hysterical, while driving in circles just trying to get them both to sleep. I was exhausted. My dad said to me, 'Get him home, you need your husband.' It had gone too far, they were concerned for my mental well-being, for their grandchildren, and they wanted him home. For the first time in our relationship he flew home early for us. With all our ups and downs, I couldn't have loved him more than I did then.

I somehow survived the first year of being a mum of two. It

hasn't been easy, I honestly don't know what it is with boys. I think most FIFO wives will say, 'It always happens when he's gone.' My two are crazy! I never know what they have in store for me. I have come out to my youngest, who was two at the time, using a knife to open a small packet of water beads. I think he thought they were 100s & 1000s. They were all over the floor and his hand was shoveling them into his mouth. I rushed to him, trying to scoop my fingers in his mouth to get them all out, frantically Googling 'what happens if you ingest water beads.' I'm not sure how many times previous to this instance I had rang the poisons hotline. Most days I think I'm a shit mum, but to have poisons on speed dial, definitely doesn't make you feel great. A whole tub of vitamins one time, drinking liquid antihistamine another time, going to the hospital after taking who knows how many adult Phenergan tablets and waiting six hours with the two of them in case he overdosed. Every single time, my husband was away. Later that night whilst getting my children ready for bed I stripped my two-year-old of his nappy to find it full of brown marble-sized balls, it took me a while to comprehend what I was seeing rolling out of his nappy on to the floor, when it suddenly clicked, the water beads had expanded in his belly and were pooped out in what was a brown squishy mess.

> **Misconception #3:** 'You can just go residential,' sign us up! If you can get us a residential job that still covers our bills, we'd be there in a heartbeat.

FIFO has definitely tested us. I am not the same bubbly, carefree girl I once was. I still have days where I resent the shit out of my husband. I feel bored, uninspired, unappreciated. I feel like my life now revolves around two little beings who trash the joint and never listen. I can go days without talking to another adult. It's lonely, it's sad, it's mundane. I know though that what my husband does for us is a sacrifice like no other - to walk out our front door every month, kiss his wife and kids goodbye and to do it for us ... is completely selfless. I am truly so proud of him and I do know that he is proud of me for how I look after and raise our children. We have just booked our third wedding to each other for our ten-year anniversary in 2022. We fight, we make up, we love each other, we dislike each other, but for us, it always has been that 'we work better together.' I can't wait for the day where we can wake up next to each other and know he doesn't have to fly-out again.

CONCLUSION

By Boris Walter (BPsychCouns)
Counsellor, Hypnotist, Life Regression Therapist,
Offshore Boilermaker/Welder

One overarching, helpful takeaway from these shared stories is that FIFO is not 'good' nor 'bad.' FIFO is an objective label for a type of work necessary for an objective outcome ... it just is. Humans engage in this type of work subjectively and uniquely, meaning everyone's story, experience, and results are different. Each worker, partner, friend or family member creates their own meaning out of their experience. The idea of an individually unique experience with FIFO life emphasises everyone's necessity to take *personal responsibility* for determining what aspects of FIFO are 'good' and/or 'bad.' You could wait for the organisational psychologists to change the companies' operating system and policies that mandate optimal ways to engage their employees. However, while you're waiting for the perfect conditions, there is something that you know you can do right now to make your life a little bit better than it was yesterday. The ideal conditions will likely never come.

Always keep in the back of one's mind, it is YOU that is engaging with the world – like watching a movie and deciding what to watch, what meaning to attribute to the experience, and what one should watch next. You have more responsibility for outcomes than you may want to admit. Start by clearly defining what it is that you want in life!

Regardless of industry, one should reset and begin with decisions based on the questions layered in the order below:

- What is good for me now?

- What is good for my immediate family now?

- What is good for my extended family?

- What is good for my social circle and lifestyle?

Following a general mind-map where one has identified what is ultimately 'good' for your individual and social sphere of value, it would be ideal to contemplate deeper with such questions:

- **Intention:** *What/who is my **ideal self**, and what do they look like? What would they be doing? How would they be acting?* This is a calling to imagining the best version of you, whether five, ten or fifty years from now.

- *Where do I find **meaning** in my life?*

- If it is work, great. You don't have to worry about emotional burn-out. But what are the effects on the family and your long-term intentions?

- If there is no meaning found at work, *where do I find my purpose of living?*

- *Can my work* **sustain me over time?** *If so, how much time?* You must have a meaningful goal to maintain yourself over time, otherwise, you run the risk of social, psychological, emotional and physical decay. Be bold in your pursuits!

SELF-KNOWLEDGE

Don't avoid your truth! There are things that you know you need to look at right now. One of your primary goals in life is to KNOW WHO YOU ARE and WHO YOU ARE NOT. There are things you know that are blocking you from living a meaningful life and having meaningful relationships at home and work. If the roster, pay, lifestyle, physical demands, or separation from home is causing you grief and negative emotions, **negotiate, communicate,** and **address it!**

Humans have an underlying motivation to be of utility to the community (we want to feel like we matter and can be of use). If you seek to be the best version of yourself for your family and friends, you have to know yourself better. If you don't know how to do this, employ a tool, method, or person of knowledge to aid you in your journey (counsellor/therapist/coach).

You have created many identities across your lifespan. Drawing upon all the accessible resources and previous experiences to inform you, you acted based on what you thought was best at the time. As you engage with the FIFO lifestyle challenges, you present yourself and act based on many underlying variables – self-worth, financial constraints, beliefs about the world, social status, previous trauma, social phobias, expectations and future intentions. These variables help to create a social character (or mask). Everybody has a social intelligence that will help them adapt to ever-changing social environments in which the mask is employed. The mask you wear at work will be different to the mask you wear at home with friends and acquaintances. The question is, who is the *real* you under all the masks? And how long can you don the mask without it becoming too heavy or losing your true self to the mask's identity?

Just like your fingerprint, your experience and the meaning you make out of those experiences are unique. That which is unique is valuable. Treat your body and life as if it is the most valuable thing in the world, and do what is necessary. Not what is easy!

PURSUE THE SELF-IDEAL

A dlerian psychology has provided grounds for over 100 years that we humans are fundamentally goal-driven – striving to the self-ideal. The self-ideal is a fictitious idea of whom we could evolve to be. If we are constantly evolving and driven to the idea that we think we are, we should get serious in adjusting our self-ideal. You are either evolving as a product of your environment with little agency or evolving into something you are authoring. One of the main reasons we 'go with the wind' and hope for the best is because we are not clear on what we want. We barely know if what we want is truly going to give us sustained happiness or the fulfilment we think it may. So, we fail. However, if you are going to fail, you should fail on *your* terms to the degree you can extract the most meaning, learning, and growth.

Hence, we have provided our readers with a self-authoring protocol that will help you clarify what you want, what drives those choices, and whether it is aimed at something meaningful. It covers all areas of the basic human psychological and existential needs. Completing this exercise will make you think about yourself as an author and lead character in your own book of life. For most of your life, you have allowed others to hold the pen and author how your life should play out. They have pushed you from the lead role to a side cameo character in your own story. It is time to grab hold of the pen and lead role and write how you want the next chapter to look and sound.

I understand it is a great responsibility to take ownership of all aspects of your life. However, if you don't adopt the necessary courage, you set yourself up for great regret, resentment and bitterness. You should be willing to die to pursue what is meaningful. Everyone in your network is counting on you.

THE SELF-IDEAL PROTOCOL

This protocol involves a set of serious questions that will get you to think about your self-other relationships in a meaningful way. The questions are designed to invoke deep reflective thought about where you stand relative to your ideals. It covers four domains of your existence: Love, Belongingness, Work, and Health. Answer these as honestly as you possibly can. Take the answers as deep, and long as you want, where reflection is invoked. If the questions require actionable goals, follow the SMART parameters (George T. Doran).

Keep the answers ...
Specific
Measurable
Achievable
Relevant
Time-bound

LOVE

Love is the energy that drives us to take on hardship and influence us towards something greater than we are.

SELF-LOVE
1. Do I deserve to be loved? Why/why not?
2. Do I take care of others better than I take care of myself? Why?
3. If I was to love myself as much as I love the person I care for most, would I treat myself differently? How?

ROMANTIC
Select the subheading that defines your current relationship status.

SINGLE PERSON
1. What am I seeking in the person I want a relationship with? (eg. Humour, honesty, business owner, facial hair, loves RnB music, etc.)
2. Do I know why I am attracted to those elements?
3. Is it time to get into a relationship? Consider elements of yourself you think you should work on.
4. Are you uncomfortable with the idea of being single? Why?

IN A RELATIONSHIP
1. Does the person I am with make me want to be better? (Encouraging, complimentary)
2. Am I okay with the shortcomings of my partner, or am I waiting for them to change?
3. If the relationship was better, what would it look like? And, what is something that would better the relationship?

BELONGING
Humans cannot be completely separate from a group. You should find yourself amongst a group of people that encourage new thought or behaviour that brings you closer to your self-ideal.

INTEREST GROUPS
1. Am I involved with a group of people who share my interests and push me to get better?
2. If not, what area of this vast world of knowledge and activities am I drawn towards?
3. What personal qualities do I want to adopt? What type of people display that quality, and how can I meet with them?

FRIENDS
1. What do I look for in friends?
2. Does the group of friends I spend most of my time with make me better and genuinely want to see me succeed?
3. Do I find myself trying too hard around them? Is it an effort around them?
4. Are the conversations stimulating?

FAMILY
1. Is there something I need to say to someone?
2. If I knew someone in my family was dying, what would I change about the relationship?
3. What can I do to make my time with my children more meaningful?
4. Am I holding a grudge, guilt, shame associated with someone in my family?
5. Is there anything regarding my family involvement that I think I will regret on my death bed?

WORK

Finding yourself of use to your community or society is a basic psychological need and a necessary life task according to pioneering psychologist, Alfred Adler.

STUDY

1. Am I learning anything new that will help me be better?
2. What is something I have wanted to learn about but never found the time?
3. If time or money wasn't an issue, what would you learn about?

CAREER

1. Is my work currently creating ongoing stress?
2. Do I wake up and dread going to work?
3. Is there some value I can draw from my work?
4. If money wasn't a factor, what would I most want to be spending my time doing as a job?
5. What is stopping me from doing that, and is it truly stopping you?
6. What would it take for that obstacle to shift and allow you to follow that ideal line of work?

HEALTH

Attitude, mindset, meaning and perceptions are emotionally linked to stress. Stress is chemically linked to disease. Disease is biologically linked to your physical health. Physical health is linked to your time on this earth.

PHYSICAL

DIET

1. What is one thing I could change about what I eat and drink that is not serving me for good?
2. What is stopping me from doing it now? Is it justified?

EXERCISE

1. What is one exercise that I could start tomorrow that I know would make a positive difference in my life if executed over the long-term?

MENTAL

MINDSET

Self-schemas – absolute statements about yourself. What are the statements you say about yourself everyday? Eg:

1. I am the author of my life
2. When I decide something, it happens
3. The universe conspires against me
4. I don't need anyone in my life
5. I'm the type of person that …
6. I don't belong in this group
7. Hardship makes me stronger
8. I can't work twelve-hour shifts
9. If only that event didn't happen to me, then I would be better off (think of more absolute statements that you make about yourself)

TRAUMAS

We are not supposed to perpetually punish ourselves from previous events, only allow ourselves to feel what is necessary and make meaning out of it.

1. What destructive patterns can I see in my life? – relationships, work …
2. What is happening in my life now that looks very similar to conditions of childhood?
3. Is my negative emotion (anger, jealousy, frustration, anxiety) a product of the current events or something deeper? Explore …

4. What is the negative emotion stopping me from feeling or doing?
5. Is there any unresolved conflict I am aware of from the past (either 1 week ago, or 20 years ago)?
6. Do I blame a person/other people for my current misfortunes? Who, and why? Is it truly beneficial to hold the resentment?
7. What would my life look like if I was able to make sense and move past the grip of the trauma?

EMOTIONAL
People attempt to control expression. Based on your self-imposed judgement, and for whatever reason, what emotions are you …
Allowed to feel? Not allowed to feel?

BEHAVIOURAL
VIRTUES
(Compassion, honesty, integrity, loyalty, etc.)
1. Have I sacrificed moral behaviour for personal gain? How and why?
2. If I treated others how I wanted to be treated, what would I change about my behaviour?

SPIRITUAL
FAITH
1. Do I believe in something greater than myself? (Creative force, God, nature, spirit guides etc.)
If so, or if not, why?

EXPLORING THE UNKNOWN
1. Am I engaging in new things?
2. Do I avoid new things?

LOVE

SELF

ROMANTIC

WORK

STUDY

CAREER

BELONGING

FRIENDS

FAMILY

BELONGING

who are you grateful for and why?

HEALTH

DIET

EXERCISE

HEALTH

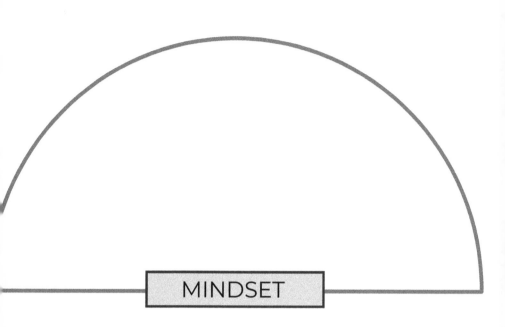

MINDSET

TRAUMAS

EMOTIONAL

HEALTH

SPIRITUAL

behavioural

Hi,
I'm Azélia.

Student by day. Author by night.

Azélia Walter is a 6 year old who loves creating. She spends most of her leisure time drawing, painting, cutting, and gluing. She also loves story time before bed, and now, she reads to her younger sister (that's if the younger sister isn't trying to rip the pages in the meantime).

Many times, Azélia would come out of her room and surprise her parents with books that she had made from paper and staples or sticky tape. The content would always be of her family or animals she wants to have as pets.

Gentle with her approach, Azélia is passionate about helping her family, friends and animals. This combined with her love of learning and teaching (again to her younger sister who has to play the student) it was only necessary, that she should be given the opportunity to explore her love for books from printing paper and staples, to the real thing and share her love with the world.

The Adventures
of a FIFO kid.

Fly out day is never fun! Luckily for these kids, they have discovered some fun adventures to go on whilst their parent is away working FIFO jobs.

According to the author, Azélia Walter (6), the real adventures begin when you are missing someone special.

Buy Now

www.theadventuresofafifokid.com
@onelittleauthor

SUPPORT RESOURCES

Sometimes life is good. And sometimes life is not so good.

The FIFO lifestyle is so rewarding. And the FIFO lifestyle is also so disheartening.

We go through ups and we go through downs. This is your reminder that those feelings are normal. It's okay to feel that way. It certainly isn't rainbows and unicorns everyday, especially in the life of a FIFO wife.

Please know that you are not alone. You do not need to suffer with your thoughts alone, reach out to someone you trust or contact one of the organisations below.

'They say it takes a village to raise a child ... however it takes a strong home unit and a bottle of wine to support a FIFO family'

FIFO Focused

www.miningfm.com
www.myfifofamily.com
www.fifofocus.com.au
www.thefifowife.com.au
www.fifolifemobileapp.com

General Helplines

www.lifeline.org.au
www.blackdoginstitute.org.au
www.beyondblue.org.au
www.mindspot.org.au
www.suicidecallbackservice.org.au
www.relationships.org.au
www.headspace.org.au
www.sane.org
www.mensline.org.au
www.talkspace.com
www.legalaid.wa.gov.au
www.gamblinghelponline.org.au
www.adf.org.au

Relationships/Family

www.familyrelationships.gov.au
www.1800respect.org.au
www.raisingchildren.net.au
www.servicesaustralia.gov.au
www.safehelpline.org
www.centrecare.com.au
www.anglicarewa.org.au
www.kidshelpline.com.au

Domestic and Family Violence

www.iamsheree.com.au
www.centreforwomen.org.au
www.zontahouse.org.au
www.womenscouncil.com.au
www.patgilescentre.org.au

www.victimsofcrime.wa.gov.au
www.dcp.wa.gov.au
www.dvconnect.org
www.whfs.org.au
Child abuse helpline 1800 199 008

Facebook Groups
The FIFO Wives' Support Group
FIFOworkerswifespartners
FIFOwivesclub
FIFOwivesclubAustralia
FIFOworkerswivespartnersopenup
FIFOLife
TheFIFOWives